RtI
for Gifted
Students

A CEC-TAG Educational Resource

Library of Congress Cataloging-in-Publication Data

RTI for gifted students : a CEG-TAG educational resource / edited by Mary Ruth Coleman and Susan K. Johnsen.
   p. cm.
  ISBN 978-1-59363-488-9 (pbk.)
  1. Remedial teaching. 2. School failure--Prevention. 3. Response to intervention (Learning disabled children) I. Coleman, Mary Ruth. II. Johnsen, Susan K.
  LB1029.R4R73 2011
  371.95'6--dc22
               2010040163

Edited by Jennifer Robins

Cover Design by Marjorie Parker
Layout Design by Raquel Trevino

ISBN-13: 978-1-59363-488-9

Printed in the United States of America.

At the time of this book's publication, all facts and figures cited are the most current available. All telephone numbers, addresses, and websites URLs are accurate and active. All publications, organizations, websites, and other resources exist as described in the book, and all have been verified. The editors and Prufrock Press Inc. make no warranty or guarantee concerning the information and materials given out by organizations or content found at websites, and we are not responsible for any changes that occur after this book's publication. If you find an error, please contact Prufrock Press Inc.

Prufrock Press Inc.
P.O. Box 8813
Waco, TX 76714-8813
Phone: (800) 998-2208
Fax: (800) 240-0333
http://www.prufrock.com

RtI

for Gifted
Students

A CEC-TAG Educational Resource

Edited by
Mary Ruth Coleman, Ph.D.,
and Susan K. Johnsen, Ph.D.

Series Editors
Cheryll M. Adams, Ph.D., Tracy L. Cross, Ph.D.,
Susan K. Johnsen, Ph.D., and Diane Montgomery, Ph.D.

PRUFROCK PRESS INC.
WACO, TEXAS

Table of Contents

List of Tables

List of Figures

Preface

Mary Ruth Coleman and Susan K. Johnsen, Editors

This book is part of a special series from The Association for the Gifted (TAG), a division within the Council for Exceptional Children. All of the contributing authors in this volume provided articles for the *Gifted Child Today* (Summer 2009) special issue on Response to Intervention (RtI); these were used as the foundation for this book.

RtI for Gifted Students focuses on the topic of Response to Intervention, particularly ways of serving gifted learners within the RtI process. In this book we have tried to balance theory, practice, and policy to present a well-rounded view of what we know and need to know about the implications of RtI for gifted learners.

The opening chapter, "Response to Intervention for Gifted Learners" by Mary Ruth Coleman, Claire E. Hughes, and Karen Rollins, offers an overview of RtI models and principles, a tiered approach to supports and services, and how gifted students and students with high potential who have not yet been formally identified might fit within different tiers of instruction. Tier 1 instruction generally includes a validated, evidence-based program that is used with all students. Students who show advanced progress with Tier 1 instruction receive collaborative interventions—Tier 2. Tier 3 instruction is for those students who need comprehensive interventions and most often involves referral to specialized services. The chapter also emphasizes the importance of early intervention to ensure that problems are prevented and strengths are not diminished.

The second chapter, "State RtI Models for Gifted Children" by Karen Rollins, Chrystyna V. Mursky, and Susan K. Johnsen, describes emerging state models that have included gifted education. One of the state models, Wisconsin, is described in detail; short summaries are provided for the other three: Colorado, Ohio, and Utah.

The third chapter, "Remembering the Importance of Potential: Tiers 1 and 2" by Mary Ruth Coleman and Sneha Shah-Coltrane, addresses the importance of nurturing potential within gifted education and describes the *U-STARS~PLUS* model. This model is centered in the K–3 regular education classroom and services all students with high-end learning opportunities, hands-on/inquiry-based science instruction, dynamic assessment, and a systematic whole-class-to-individual observation of potential.

Within the fourth chapter, "Addressing the Needs of Students Who Are Twice-Exceptional" by Daphne Pereles, Lois Baldwin, and Stuart Omdal, take a close look at how the use of RtI, which began as an alternative approach to identifying students with learning disabilities, works for students who are twice-exceptional. This chapter shares a case study to illustrate how RtI might impact a child who is twice-exceptional, showing the possibilities for earlier supports and services to set children on a trajectory for success.

Next, we examine policy issues in the fifth chapter, "RtI for Gifted Students: Policy Implications" by Elissa F. Brown and Sherry H. Abernethy. This chapter offers solid guidance for decision makers faced with the implications of using RtI approaches with gifted students. The authors, who are state consultants, describe potential RtI components for gifted policy development and the implementation of RtI within North Carolina.

The sixth chapter, "Assessing Your School's RtI Model in Serving Gifted Students" by Susan K. Johnsen, provides a way to determine if a school's RtI model would provide for gifted and talented students by examining the overall model, how student progress is monitored, tiers of service, curriculum and instructional practices, and collaboration. This chapter provides specific questions to ask and the knowledge and skills associated with gifted, general, and special educator roles.

In the seventh chapter, we take a look at the remaining challenges with "Challenges for Including Gifted Education Within an RtI Model" by Claire E. Hughes, Karen Rollins, Susan K. Johnsen, Daphne A. Pereles, Stuart Omdal, Lois Baldwin, Elissa F. Brown, Sherry H. Abernethy, and Mary Ruth Coleman. These challenges include RtI as systemic change, implementing RtI in schools and classrooms, and specific implementation issues for twice-exceptional students.

Finally, we provide an annotated listing of websites that have resources for implementing Response to Intervention. These sites provide a wealth of materials that include assessments, activities, lesson plans, behavior management techniques, research, and much more.

We hope that this book will be useful to the field as we explore together the possibilities of RtI for gifted learners.

CHAPTER 1

Response to Intervention for Gifted Learners

Claire E. Hughes, Karen Rollins, and Mary Ruth Coleman

The Response to Intervention (RtI) model is sweeping the country, changing the way children's educational needs are recognized and met. RtI was introduced through special education legislation as part of the Individuals with Disabilities Education Improvement Act (IDEA, 2004) and offered an alternative approach for identifying students with learning disabilities (Bender & Shores, 2007). Its impact today, however, has moved well beyond this initial goal (Council for Exceptional Children, 2007). RtI is designed to bring together information about each child's strengths and needs with evidence-based instructional approaches that support the child's success (Kirk, Gallagher, Coleman, & Anastasiow, 2009). Although RtI is still an emerging practice, it hinges on a collaborative approach to recognizing and responding to the needs of each child. This collaborative approach requires educators to think about the child first and match the supports and services to his or her strengths and needs. The allocation of resources follows the supports and services, promoting synergy rather than increasing fragmentation, as the needs of the child increase. In other words, within the RtI model, when the child's needs are the most intense, educational resources can be combined to provide greater support. This use of resources differs significantly from traditional approaches where, as the needs of the child intensify, the supports and services become more separate and rigidly codified with clear boundaries delineating the allocation of resources.

A comprehensive approach to RtI addresses the needs of all learners, including learners who need additional time, support, practice, and/or more intense direct instruction to meet with success *and* learners who need more challenge and a faster pace of learning to meet with success. This comprehensive approach encompasses all learners and helps educators remember to address students' strengths as we work to meet their needs. When students with gifts and talents are left out of the framework, their needs are not addressed, and they often do not make the academic gains they are capable of accomplishing. This is particularly true for students from low socioeconomic (low-SES) backgrounds who may need early support to prevent academic declines (Wyner, Bridgeland, & DiIulio, 2007). Within a comprehensive approach to RtI, attention is given to maintaining academic progress for all learners at the highest possible level.

MODELS OF IMPLEMENTATION

The strategies used to address learners' needs (for both curriculum enhancement and for additional support) fall into two major approaches: the use of standard protocols and the use of a problem-solving process. Each approach has different implications when used for addressing the needs of students with gifts and talents.

THE STANDARD PROTOCOL MODEL

The standard protocol model requires the use of scientifically based classroom instruction for all students using the same curriculum, the same program, and/or the same management strategies; regular administration of curriculum-based assessments; and frequent comparisons of students to expected or normal growth (Fuchs & Fuchs, 2005). Standard protocols that address learners' needs are identified and defined ahead of time so that they are "ready on the right" when teachers see students with specific sets of needs. Because standard protocols are well-defined interventions (they may even be scripted), it is relatively easy to help practitioners use an intervention correctly with large numbers of students. The goal of standard protocols is to ensure that all learners receive optimum instruction to help them make appropriate progress.

Fuchs and Fuchs (2005) described an elementary school that used a standard protocol RtI model for students with reading difficulties. For screening, each first-grade student was administered a curriculum-based measurement word identification fluency assessment (CBM-WIF) in September. All students in Tier 1 instruction received a validated reading curriculum program. To ensure that the reading program was implemented correctly, the school's lead reading teacher observed each first-grade teacher's classroom quarterly. The teachers kept records that monitored each student's progress. Students who were not learning approximately 1.75 words per week then received Tier 2 instruction. In Tier 2, students received 45 minutes of instruction four times each week in groups of one to three from tutors who had completed training. The lead reading teacher also observed these tutors and provided corrective feedback. Once each week, the lead reading teacher met with all of the tutors for one hour to examine the students' CBM-WIF graphs and to problem solve about students whose progress was inadequate. Tutoring sessions then focused on specific areas of student weakness that included phonological awareness, letter-sound recognition, decoding, sight word recognition, short story reading with highly explicit instruction, and self-regulated learning strategies to increase motivation and goal-directed learning. In this model, the third tier was referral to special education, which included a comprehensive evaluation phase. Across all tiers, teams empirically set decision rules to plan changes based on past research with specific interventions.

When we think of the needs of students who are gifted, we must reframe the standard protocol interventions so that they offer additional enrichment, challenge, and enhancement for learners with strengths in the targeted area (e.g., reading, as in the case above). For students whose progress monitoring data indicate a strength in reading, standard protocols might include:

- curriculum compacting to release students from additional direct instruction and guided and independent practice on skills where they have shown mastery;
- selection of advanced reading material on the students' independent reading levels that allow them to keep reading logs with key questions in their journals;
- participation in seminar discussion with other students who are reading the same level material; and
- learning opportunities that allow students to explore their interests in more depth.

In summary, the standard protocol RtI model uses a high-quality, research-based, standardized curriculum in Tier 1; monitors students to identify those who need additional support or enhancement to meet with optimal success; provides for collaboration among special and general educators; and refers to specialized services in Tier 3 if the student needs additional support for success (New Mexico Public Education Department, 2008). Although the standard protocol is used primarily for children who may need additional support for success in reading, it should also be used with children who are advanced in reading if the standard curriculum can be differentiated.

THE PROBLEM-SOLVING MODEL

The problem-solving approach relies on a system of increasingly intensive interventions that are planned and implemented by school personnel to provide an effective program for a particular student (Deno, 2002; Mellard, Byrd, Johnson, Tollefson, & Boesche, 2004). The four-level problem-solving model generally involves (a) identifying the problem, (b) designing and implementing interventions, (c) monitoring the student's progress and modifying the interventions according to the student's responsiveness, and (d) planning the next steps. Because each child's needs are addressed individually, professional expertise and collaborative consultation are essential for success.

The Minneapolis Public Schools used a three-stage problem-solving model (Hegranes, Casey, & Marston, 2006). The problem-solving steps included (a) problem identification, (b) problem definition, (c) designing intervention plans, (d) implementing interventions, and (e) problem solution. In Stage 1, classroom intervention, the teacher identified specific concerns and baseline data were collected for an individual student. Other relevant information such as school history and relevant health issues was collected from the student, parents, and staff members. Classroom modifications were then made and the student's progress was documented for 4–6 weeks. Following this modification and perhaps other modifications, the student may have entered Stage 2. At this stage, a team of educators provided research-based intervention strategies and ideas to the general education teacher.

In this model, in addition to the general education teacher, the team may include a Title I teacher, counselor, social worker, psychologist, speech and language pathologist, special education teacher(s), and building administrator. When the team is addressing the needs of a student who is gifted and talented, the gifted education specialist should also participate. The team establishes a goal and an intervention is selected. To maintain the integrity of the intervention, activities are monitored and documented. These data are then used to document student progress and evaluate the effectiveness of the suggested interventions, approximately 6–8 weeks later. The team then decides to continue the intervention, to modify the intervention, or to refer the student for special education evaluation—Stage 3.

In summary, the problem-solving RtI model uses varied curriculum and multiple interventions, monitors students to identify those who may need additional supports and enhancement, provides for collaboration among a range of educators, and refers to special and or gifted education services if the suggested interventions show a need for additional support.

PRINCIPLES OF RESPONSE TO INTERVENTION

Regardless of the approach used, if education is to focus on developing student abilities, then it must also focus on the growth and achievement for all students—where *all* truly does mean *all*. In the face of changing educational policies and processes, such as RtI, it is critically important that teachers and advocates for gifted education come to the table to ensure that the philosophy that undergirds the changes inherent in the law are addressed to meet the needs of all students. From a practical viewpoint, this means that gifted education will also need to shift as there are some critical areas that may look somewhat different within an RtI framework.

Key components of RtI include: (a) a tiered or stage approach to supports and services; (b) early intervention prior to formal identification; (c) universal screening, (d) fidelity of implementation through standard protocol interventions, (e) progress monitoring or dynamic assessments to determine the child's needs and to plan instruction; (f) the use of professional development so that practitioners can implement the interventions; and (g) collaborative problem-solving structures that allow (h) greater involvement with parents.

Table 1.1 summarizes the major RtI principles (Council for Exceptional Children, The Association for the Gifted [CEC-TAG], 2009; Fuchs & Deshler, 2007; Fuchs & Fuchs, 2007) and describes how they would change gifted education. The remainder of this chapter will explore what gifted education might look like within an RtI framework.

THE TIERED APPROACH TO SUPPORTS AND SERVICES

The use of tiered approaches to supporting strengths is not new for gifted education. The field has relied on curriculum differentiation strategies that promote tiered lessons and units for many years (Tomlinson, 1999). Gifted students are an incredibly heterogeneous group (Cross, 2005), with greater diversity in achievement levels than among typical students. Thus, the idea of a one-size-fits-all gifted education program is not based upon the actual characteristics of gifted students. Historically, there has often been a disconnect between the process of identification (based upon characteristics of gifted students) and the program that is offered for gifted learners (Coleman & Gallagher, 1995). In a tiered framework, teachers would be better able to meet the needs of gifted

TABLE 1.1
RTI PRINCIPLES AND IMPLICATIONS FOR SERVING THE NEEDS OF GIFTED STUDENTS

RTI Principle	Traditional Gifted Education	Gifted Education Within RTI
Tiered system of interventions	The more intense the needs, the more intense and long-term the instructional intervention and the more different the learning environment; many "one-size-fits-all" programs versus services	Scaffolding support that starts with differentiation in Tier 1, targeted support for strengths in Tier 2, and individualized supports in Tier 3 (formal identification may take place here)
Early intervention	Supporting learners in the general education program, with formal identification at grades 2 or 3	Recognizing ability within a nurturing system regardless of label and providing early support to develop potential for all learners
Universal screening	Establishing scores that students would reach to be placed in the "talent pool"	Establishing scores that students would reach that indicate a need for differentiated and advanced instruction
Fidelity of intervention	Reviewing and evaluating programming to examine parental and student satisfaction and effectiveness of program	Reviewing and evaluating programming to ensure that the student actually receives instruction geared to his or her particular needs—not a "one-size-fits-all" gifted program; using student outcome data to show that growth has taken place
Progress monitoring	Using some preassessment and curriculum compacting to allow students to show mastery	Documenting student progress with a goal of providing the appropriate level of instruction to match the student's strengths, interests, and pace of learning
Professional development	Providing specific, research-based interventions that are appropriate for the needs of the child	Providing specific strategies of acceleration, enrichment, and differentiation that are effective with gifted learners

TABLE 1.1, CONTINUED

Collaborative structure	Collaborating when needed and time permits	Collaborating between gifted, special, and general education teachers to identify and serve high-achieving students in need of differentiated services; providing greater possibilities for twice-exceptional students
Parental involvement	Sharing information with and from families to look at achievement levels and effectiveness of interventions	Collaborating with families to look at achievement levels and effectiveness of interventions; building targeted interventions based on information regarding each student's interest areas and areas of strength

learners based on their individual characteristics by differentiating within the group of gifted students. Even though students may have been identified as gifted, there are still strengths, weaknesses, and a tremendous range of actual performance levels within this group.

Important aspects to remember within the tiers of instruction are the concepts of flexibility and fluidity. Once a student has been identified as needing a different tier of instruction, whether it is for remediation or enrichment, it is imperative to allow that child the flexibility of movement as he or she develops in the area of need. Also, in respect to movement, fluidity allows that child to move within tiers when needed. With students who need additional time, practice, and exposure to meet with success, this movement may be advancing to another tier for more specific instruction and then returning to a previous tier once specific concepts have been mastered. This cycle of movement is based on progress monitoring data, and additional support is provided when needed. With a gifted child, the same fluidity of movement is important. A gifted student may require supports at the higher level tier indefinitely based on the intensity of his or her strengths.

The tiered approach within RtI extends this thinking to the supports and services provided. What this might look like in each service tier is briefly presented below.

TIER 1

In Tier 1, the general education classroom offers a quality learning environment, nurtures all children with a focus on high-end learning opportunities, uses dynamic assessments including whole-class screenings for potential, and uses standardized progress monitoring to document children's mastery of the curriculum. The general education teacher is responsible for supports and differentiation. Tier 1 includes instruction that would be differentiated within the general education classroom. Using differentiation methods recommended by gifted education experts such as Kaplan, Tomlinson, and VanTassel-Baska, students would have the opportunity within the general education classroom to excel and strive for higher levels.

TIER 2

Tier 2 involves a collaborative approach that provides additional supports and learning opportunities for children based on strengths and needs. It responds to each child based on data showing evidence of strengths, needs, and interests; provides supports (often to small groups of children) within the general classroom setting; administers individual assessments to understand the child's strengths; develops plans for differentiated instruction; and uses a standard protocol to offer additional challenges and high-end learning opportunities. Collaboration between the general and gifted education teachers is essential, with parents being included in the discussion of the child's strengths and weaknesses. In Tier 2, perhaps using the assistance of a gifted education teacher, students would receive additional enrichment and/or accelerative options within specific content areas. Contracts and compacting are strategies that could be employed to provide challenging instruction in those areas of strength for a gifted child.

TIER 3

In Tier 3, more intense and individualized services are provided to meet the needs of the child. Assessments, including additional information regarding the child's strengths and a body of evidence (including standardized measures), are complied to look at the child's needs. Nomination for formal identification is considered, and parents are included in the decision making. The gifted education specialist may take the lead at this point. In Tier 3, perhaps the most intensive services, gifted students would receive more significant acceleration and/or gifted group activities. The criteria for such programming would be based on clearly established protocols such as those developed for acceleration practices (Colangelo, Assouline, & Gross, 2004). Examples of Tier 3 services include intensive acceleration, such as skipping a grade, early Advanced Placement (AP) classes, or early college classes.

A increasing levels of instruction and student achievement levels rise, off-level testing will be required to measure progress. A child who scores in the 95th or 99th percentile on a standardized test when compared to his or her peers has "topped" out the test. The full range of that child's knowledge or skills is still not known to teachers. Similarly, a student who scores 100 on a curriculum-based measure or a pretest before instruction has clearly mastered that level of curriculum, but it is still not clear the level of his or her achievement. In order to provide such information, it is necessary to use tests and measures that are designed for an above-grade-level population to know each child's actual level of performance. This will help teachers know where to begin teaching. Programs such as the Study of Mathematically Precocious Youth (SMPY) have been organized around this principle for years. If educators were to teach students at their actual levels of achievement, rather than where we think they should be, much of the charges of elitism and other negative aspects of gifted or special education programming would simply vanish.

EARLY INTERVENTION TO SUPPORT THE CHILD'S STRENGTHS

The focus of RtI is on early intervention, the early provision of services that build on the child's strengths and address his or her learning needs. Early intervention is critical in order to prevent problems, to mitigate the impact of existing problems, and to ensure that strengths do not diminish. Early intervention generally focuses on remediation to shore up areas of weakness for the child. For a gifted child, however, the early intervention focuses on nurturing potential to support the child's areas of strength. With the RtI approach, early intervention can begin as soon as the strengths of the child are recognized—often well before the child is formally identified as gifted. In this way, the child's strengths are nurtured during the first years of schooling, building a strong platform for his or her continued success. In many schools, formal identification of giftedness does not take place until the end of second or third grade; thus, young children with high potential are left with little to no additional support. Early recognition of and response to the child's strengths is important for all children, but it is essential for young gifted children from culturally/linguistically diverse and economically disadvantaged families. The focus on early nurturing of potential helps to ensure that each child is placed on a trajectory for maximum success.

Often, gifted education is reserved for students who qualify for gifted services; however, many students may not score above a required cut-off point without some exposure to specific content and/or proper identification. In a case for early intervention, the issue of nurturing talent, especially among diverse populations, becomes primary. Many students enter schools with lower achievement because of extenuating circumstances that impact their level of achievement in a mainstream classroom. By waiting to provide talent development activities until students "qualify" for gifted education services, schools are ensuring that only students whose strengths have been nurtured prior to entering school are identified. RtI promises an exciting means of nurturing talent and the potential for growth before a student officially qualifies for services.

In addition, there are many instances where students are not identi-fied as gifted due to a "mismatch" between the identification instrument and the child's strengths. By implementing an RtI delivery model that incorporates tiers for students performing above their peers in the school curriculum, educators can ensure that all students with potential receive services—even those who do not qualify for gifted services using the des-ignated instrument of choice from the district. Without nurturing the strengths of gifted students, true growth cannot occur, and students are in danger of not developing—and even losing—their gifts.

Most significantly, by allowing the integrated opportunities for enrichment and remediation, the needs of twice-exceptional students can be more easily met. Winebrenner (2003) suggested that when work-ing with twice-exceptional students, teachers should give direct instruc-tion of needed skills while providing acceleration and enrichment, with emphasis on problem solving, reasoning, and critical thinking. Such dual-instructional approaches become possible when gifted education, special education, and general education teachers are working together to provide instruction that matches each child's curricular needs. For example, a child might score in the 90th percentile in math, and in the 20th percentile in reading. That child could conceivably have both needs met by different tiers of instruction: advanced instruction in math with reading modifications and direct instruction in reading strategies.

UNIVERSAL SCREENING

To implement RtI with gifted students, universal screening needs to include all students who are achieving at a high level. Using a paral-lel structure to traditional RtI, those students who score in the top 25% could warrant extra attention (e.g., additional challenges or differentiated instruction). Students in the top 5% to 10% of the class would need sig-nificantly more intensive interventions. In addition, universal screening needs to include assessments that are above grade level so that exceptional students who might be candidates for significant acceleration in certain subject areas are identified.

As a member of an RtI team within a school, it would be important to have two discussion points: those students performing below given criteria and those students performing above a certain criteria.

As a school system, procedures need to be in place to identify children who are performing either significantly above or significantly below their peers. Because of ceiling effects found among students who score in the 90th percentile and above and floor effects from students who score below the 15th percentile, testing procedures should allow specialists to offer off-grade-level testing to determine at what grade level a student is actually performing. A fifth grader who is scoring above the 95th percentile in math might be performing at a seventh-grade level, or even at a ninth-grade level. Similarly, a fifth-grade student who scores at the 10th percentile in math might be performing at the first-grade level. For instructional planning, it would be important to know specific knowledge and skills needed for both students.

FIDELITY OF INTERVENTION

Ensuring the fidelity of intervention, or a systematic procedure that is clearly followed for all students, ensures two important aspects: (a) curricular interventions are data-based decisions and are related to identifiable, measurable gifted characteristics; and (b) educators are held accountable for presenting the instruction in a manner that reflects best teaching practices.

PROGRESS MONITORING

Progress monitoring is the systematic gathering of data to evaluate the progress of a child. For a teacher, it means knowing how one will evaluate a child on a particular set of skills over time. It may mean repeating a set of curriculum-based measures, or using a more standardized test over the course of several weeks. Progress monitoring is key to planning instruction in Tiers 1 and 2. The goal in a strengths-based RtI model is to raise achievement *beyond* the general education classroom. Heightened achievement gains that are achieved in Tier 2 should be maintained and encouraged. Progress monitoring is critical to determine how much a student's achievement levels are changing over time, with the goal being achievement gains for all students.

PROFESSIONAL DEVELOPMENT

The Higher Education Opportunity Act (2008) requires all teacher preparation programs to contain information about teaching gifted learners. The National Association for Gifted Children (NAGC) currently is examining the core knowledge that would be considered essential for general education teachers because the majority of gifted children spend most of their time in general education classrooms. Currently, there is a set of core knowledge and skills that CEC-TAG, NAGC, and the National Council for Accreditation of Teacher Education (NCATE) organizations have recently provided for the education of teachers of gifted students (Johnsen, VanTassel-Baska, & Robinson, 2008; Kitano, Montgomery, VanTassel-Baska, & Johnsen, 2008). These standards provide a set of professional development guidelines for school districts.

COLLABORATIVE STRUCTURE

Perhaps the area of greatest potential to aid the classroom teacher in using the RtI model is in the area of collaboration. Collaboration as a service delivery option currently exists in special education and holds great promise for RtI as a means of identifying and serving students who need additional interventions (Murawski & Hughes, 2009). Great potential exists for gifted educators to be tapped as resources in order to better enable the general education teacher to meet the needs of potentially gifted students. Gifted education teachers can gather data, provide ongoing assessment, and offer services for students at multiple tiers, such as acceleration and enrichment activities, to students showing a need for these services. Although research indicates that within a general education setting, little to no differentiation for high-achieving students occurs on a regular, systematic basis (Tomlinson, 2008), differentiation can occur.

In addition to the services that gifted education teachers can provide within a general education setting, they can also provide more intensive direct services in a Tier 3 setting. Some school districts may opt for accelerative or self-contained settings for gifted students who significantly exceed the achievement level of their peers and need to continue to grow and achieve. Ensuring such growth for students who are two to five grade levels ahead of their peers would require school districts to provide services that emphasize growth for all.

Finally, one of the strongest aspects of the collaborative process is the ability to meet the needs of twice-exceptional learners, or gifted students with disabilities. Twice-exceptional students are directly cited in the Individuals with Disabilities Education Act (IDEA, 1990) as a population that must have its diverse needs met. States and districts do not have the option to only meet the remedial needs of twice-exceptional students; they *must* develop the individual child's abilities as well. In fact, in the case of twice-exceptional students, it is critical to develop strengths while remediating, because remediation alone does not build self-efficacy for students with learning disabilities (Little, 2001). With the legal mandate, gifted education professionals have an opportunity to engage with special and general educators in a problem-solving process that can produce a coherent instructional approach, rather than the often disjointed educational patchwork that emerges with twice-exceptional learners (Hughes, 2009). Similarly, such opportunities for collaboration exist for gifted English language learners (ELL) and Title I populations. Providing a vehicle for collaboration through RtI can ensure the professional respect of a gifted education teacher, and consequently, the field.

PARENTAL INVOLVEMENT

One of the keys to the success of the RtI model is developing strategies that are effective for each child. In order to link content to a student, it is critical to know the interests and strengths of that particular child, whether the interventions be for remediation (Brown-Chidsey & Steege,

2005) or for enrichment nature (Reis, Burns, & Renzulli, 1992). Parents, clearly, have a valued perspective on their child's strengths and interests. In addition, the family, if it has worked with an educational system for some length of time, will have a clearer idea of strategies that have been tried and found effective with the child in the past than will a teacher developing a plan with limited experience with a child.

In addition to providing information to educators, parents also are ultimately responsible for their child's education, and as such, can glean information from educators about choices available for their child. Through teamwork, educators and parents can work together to meet the high-level needs of students who may be beyond their age peers.

FITTING RTI AND GIFTED EDUCATION TOGETHER

There are four essential determinations to make when creating a Response to Intervention plan, whether the focus is on a child who is falling behind or a child who is ahead of his or her peers. These include strategies to determine: (a) the need, (b) the intervention, (c) the progress, and (d) the decision-making criteria. Each of these four areas involves all members of the team. This team might consist of administrators, the classroom teacher, the instructional specialist, the intervention teacher, the gifted education teacher, parents, the school psychologist, the person responsible for examining student growth, or anyone else who has a vested interest in the success of the child. It is not recommended that students who are ahead of their peers have a separate process from students who are falling behind their peers. All members of the team should undertake the same challenge: "How can we assist this child in making achievement gains when the standard curriculum is not appropriate to do so?"—whether it is a struggling child or a high-achieving child.

Thinking about how gifted education fits within an RtI framework provides an opportunity to reexamine what educators believe about meeting the needs of children. These are our reflections on fitting RtI and gifted education together:

- the emphasis within RtI on early intervention or the recognition of strengths prior to formal identification reminds us of our commitment to nurture potential in all children;
- the provision of tiered responses that scaffold learning and support across general and gifted education reminds us of our commitment to excellence for all;
- the use of dynamic assessments that inform instruction reminds us of the importance of data-driven decision making;
- the use of standard protocols reminds us that rigorous curriculum is central to differentiated instruction; and
- the use of collaborative planning reminds us of the importance of partnerships with parents as we plan to meet the child's needs.

All in all, gifted education can be an excellent fit within the RtI approach that so many school systems are adopting. RtI is the means for special, general, and gifted educators to work together in developing a common goal of fitting services to each and every student. Done correctly, gifted education, using RtI, can not only advance the needs of children but also increase the number of effective research-based programs.

REFERENCES

Bender, W., & Shores, C. (2007). *Response to Intervention: A practical guide for every teacher.* Arlington, VA: Council for Exceptional Children.

Brown-Chidsey, R., & Steege, M. W. (2005). *Response to Intervention: Principles and strategies for effective practice.* New York, NY: Guilford Press.

Colangelo, N., Assouline, S. G., & Gross, M. U. M. (2004). *A nation deceived: How schools hold back America's brightest students* (Vol. 1). Iowa City: The University of Iowa, The Connie Belin & Jacqueline N. Blank International Center for Gifted Education and Talent Development.

Coleman, M. R., & Gallagher, J. (1995). State identification policies: Gifted students from special populations. *Roeper Review, 17,* 268–275.

Council for Exceptional Children. (2007). *Position on response to intervention (RTI): The unique role of special education and special educators.* Retrieved from http://www.cec.sped.org/AM/Template.cfm?Section=Home&CONTENTID=9237&TEMPLATE=/CM/ContentDisplay.cfm

Council for Exceptional Children, The Association for Gifted. (2009, April). *Response to intervention for giftedness: A position paper.* Retrieved from http://www.cectag.org

Cross, T. (2005). *The social and emotional lives of gifted kids: Understanding and guiding their development.* Waco, TX: Prufrock Press.

Deno, S. L. (2002). Problem solving as "best practice." In A. Thomas & J. Grimes (Eds.), *Best practices in school psychology IV* (pp. 37–56). Bethesda, MD: NASP.

Fuchs, D., & Deshler, D. D. (2007). What we need to know about responsiveness to intervention (and shouldn't be afraid to ask). *Learning Disabilities Research & Practice, 22,* 129–136.

Fuchs, D., & Fuchs, L. S. (2005). Responsiveness-to-Intervention: A blueprint for practitioners, policymakers, and parents. *Teaching Exceptional Children, 38,* 57–61.

Fuchs, D., & Fuchs, L. S. (Eds.). (2007). Responsiveness to intervention [Special issue]. *Teaching Exceptional Children, 39*(5).

Hegranes, T., Casey, A., & Marston, D. (2006). *Response to Intervention (RTI): 3 tiered system.* Retrieved from http://www.k8accesscenter.org/documents/RTIwebinar6-20_000.ppt

Higher Education Opportunity Act, Pub. Law 110-315 (August 14, 2008).

Hughes, C. E. (2009). Janusian gifted: Twice-exceptional children and two worlds. In B. MacFarlane & T. Stambaugh (Eds.), *Leading change in gifted education: The festschrift of Dr. Joyce VanTassel-Baska* (pp. 183–193). Waco, TX: Prufrock Press.

Individuals with Disabilities Education Act, 20 U.S.C. §1401 et seq. (1990).

Individuals with Disabilities Education Improvement Act, Pub. Law 108-446 (December 3, 2004).

Johnsen, S. K., VanTassel-Baska, J., & Robinson, A. (2008). *Using the national gifted education standards for university teacher preparation programs.* Thousand Oaks, CA: Corwin Press.

Kirk, S., Gallagher, J., Coleman, M., & Anastasiow, N. (2009). *Educating exceptional children* (12th ed.). Boston, MA: Houghton Mifflin.

Kitano, M., Montgomery, D., VanTassel-Baska, J., & Johnsen, S. (2008). *Using the national gifted education standards for PreK–12 professional development.* Thousand Oaks, CA: Corwin Press.

Little, C. (2001). A closer look at gifted children with disabilities. *Gifted Child Today, 24*(3), 46–64.

Mellard, D., Byrd, S. E., Johnson, E., Tollefson, J. M., & Boesche, L. (2004). Foundations and research on identifying model Responsiveness-to-Intervention sites. *Learning Disability Quarterly, 27,* 243–256.

Murawski, W. A., & Hughes, C. E. (2009). Response to Intervention, collaboration, and coteaching: A recipe for successful systemic change. *Preventing School Failure, 53,* 267–275.

New Mexico Public Education Department. (2008). *Response to Intervention (RTI) fact sheet.* Retrieved from http://www.ped.state.nm.us/RTI/factSheet.html

Reis, S. M., Burns, D. E., & Renzulli, J. S. (1992). *Curriculum compacting: The complete guide to modifying the regular curriculum for high ability students.* Mansfield Center, CT: Creative Learning Press.

Tomlinson, C. A. (1999). *The differentiated classroom: Responding to the needs of all learners.* Alexandria, VA: Association for Supervision and Curriculum Development.

Tomlinson, C. A. (2008). Differentiated instruction. In J. A. Plucker & C. M. Callahan (Eds.), *Critical issues and practices in gifted education: What the research says* (pp. 167–179). Waco, TX: Prufrock Press.

Winebrenner, S. (2003). *Teaching gifted kids in the regular classroom: Strategies and techniques every teacher can use to meet the academic needs of the gifted and talented.* Minneapolis, MN: Free Spirit.

Wyner, J. S., Bridgeland, J. M., & DiIulio, J. J., Jr. (2007). *Achievement trap: How America is failing millions of high-achieving students from lower-income families.* Washington, DC: Jack Kent Cooke Foundation and Civic Enterprises.

CHAPTER 2

State RtI Models for Gifted Children

Karen Rollins, Chrystyna V. Mursky, and
Susan K. Johnsen

Response to Intervention (RtI) has promise for helping students achieve higher levels of academic and behavioral success. RtI models, as discussed in Chapter 1, tend to use a problem-solving approach and incorporate (a) curriculum and instructional practices, (b) monitoring of student progress, (c) collaboration, and/or (d) tiered levels of services. Although most of the current models address only those students who are not progressing as expected, some RtI models have included gifted education. What does this model look like for students with gifts and talents or for students who are twice-exceptional, such as those who are gifted and have a learning disability? How might current RtI models be expanded to identify and support the needs of children who learn at a faster pace and require more complex curricula? In this chapter, we will discuss state RtI models that include gifted education or have the potential to do so.

RTI MODELS THAT INCLUDE STUDENTS WITH GIFTS AND TALENTS

Because the federal government does not require a specific Response to Intervention model, each state has been able to design and implement its own. Although the majority of states have focused on students with disabilities, some have designed models that include gifted education. In this section we will describe one of the state models in detail and provide short summaries of three others.

WISCONSIN

The Wisconsin Department of Public Instruction (WDPI) frames RtI as a system for meeting the needs of *all* learners. WDPI recognizes the potential RtI holds for achieving higher levels of academic and behavioral success for all students, including those whose needs extend beyond the core curriculum. The membership of the workgroup that developed the Wisconsin framework reflects this inclusive philosophy. Members hail from a variety of different WDPI teams, including Special Education, Content and Learning, Teacher Education, Professional Development and Licensing, Title I, and Student Services. Voices for all students, including those with gifts and talents, were at the table as the RtI framework was developed.

Details about Wisconsin's journey are discussed in three sections below. The first summarizes the characteristics the WDPI believes describe effective gifted education plans and then connects these characteristics to an RtI framework. The second section provides an overview of the components of the WDPI framework for RtI. The third section describes a few specific RtI models found in Wisconsin schools.

Wisconsin's framework for gifted education and RtI. The Wisconsin DPI believes that there are seven key characteristics of an effective gifted education plan:

- *Systemic*. Gifted education should be integrated into school-wide initiatives and programming across all grade levels, K–12.

Learning opportunities should be incorporated into the regular school day and the regular school year.

- *Responsive.* Gifted education should respond to local student demographics, curriculum, resources, and needs.
- *Fluid.* Gifted education should be flexible and continuously adapt to student needs.
- *Appropriate.* Gifted education should provide opportunities that are in place of, not in addition to, regular classroom instruction and activities.
- *Collaborative.* Gifted education should be the responsibility of all staff members working in a collaborative fashion to meet student needs.
- *Sustainable.* Gifted education should be an integral part of the school district's staffing and funding plans. It should not be dependent on any particular person or funding sources.
- *Comprehensive.* Gifted education should consider the "whole child" by fostering academic, social, and personal growth of the student.

If we examine these seven characteristics of effective gifted education, we can see many of the terms and ideas represented in an RtI framework as previously described in Chapter 1. First, RtI is a schoolwide initiative (i.e., systemic) for all students, including those with gifts and talents. As such, it is sustainable, and less likely to be eliminated during times of tight budgets. RtI is designed to respond to the academic and behavioral needs of students using a problem-solving model. This approach incorporates the notion of collaboration. The use of dynamic assessment in an RtI system provides comprehensive information on students in order to make instructional decisions that are appropriate. Progress monitoring ensures that an RtI framework remains fluid. It's clear, therefore, that an RtI system supports effective gifted education.

Framework components for RtI. The Wisconsin DPI believes that the concept of RtI is, on the one hand, quite simple. Using data from sound assessments, a collaborative decision-making or problem-solving approach is applied to determine if what teachers are doing is working. On the other hand, the WDPI also believes RtI is quite complex because it represents a systems change—a process that often takes 3–6 years to complete. Individual school districts in Wisconsin make many of their own curricular and assessment decisions, so the WDPI does not prescribe any particular RtI framework (such as the three-tiered model). Instead it advocates that a successful RtI system provides multiple levels of support that integrate three key components: (a) high-quality instruction, (b) continuous review of student progress, and (c) collaboration. At the heart is culturally responsive practices. This framework is represented by the graphic in Figure 2.1.

High-quality instruction. The Wisconsin DPI suggests that RtI begins with high-quality instruction that includes a rigorous curriculum and research-based effective practices. Tomlinson (2005) described several key aspects that characterize instruction such as this. She noted that it (a) focuses on rich and profound ideas of the discipline; (b) engages students emotionally and cognitively; (c) requires students to solve problems, address issues, and create products; and (d) is relevant to students' lives. The core or universal curriculum that is designed for all students reflects these characteristics, and the depth and complexity that are embedded are generally not differentiated. The specific tasks students perform related to this curriculum, however, can and should be differentiated in order to engage students and meet their needs.

Central to the success of Wisconsin's RtI framework is putting students at the center of decisions about these needs. High-quality classroom instructional practices respond to students' individual differences to help them meet academic and behavioral benchmarks. Teachers are flexible in planning learning opportunities, a concept often referred to as *differentiated instruction*. Students, however, differ in their readiness, learning profiles, interests, and talents. Learning opportunities, therefore, must be differentiated to engage each student in meaningful tasks that offer an appropriate level of challenge. Teachers adjust their instruction to respond to the needs of the learners—they do not expect the learners to adjust to their teaching. For students who are not able to meet academic and behavioral benchmarks with simple differentiation or for students who have already met or exceeded the benchmarks, high-quality instruction provides appropriate interventions. These interventions can include targeted support, scaffolding, additional practice, enrichment,

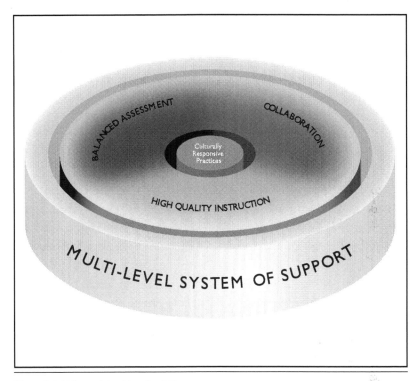

Figure 2.1. Wisconsin's vision for RtI.

compacting, or acceleration. As mentioned in Chapter 1, determining which differentiated learning opportunities or interventions best match student needs is accomplished using dynamic assessment, and evaluating the effectiveness of the opportunities and interventions is accomplished through progress monitoring.

Continuous review of student progress. The relationship between assessment and instruction is well documented. For example, Wiggins (1998) stated that school-based assessment should aim mainly to improve student performance. Danielson (2007) noted that effective teachers actively and systematically elicit information about students' understanding in order to monitor their progress and make instructional decisions. It's this link between assessment and instruction that makes it evident why the second key component in the Wisconsin DPI's RtI framework is continuous review of student progress using a balanced assessment system.

This balanced assessment system includes sound summative, bench-mark, and formative measures that Wisconsin school districts select to provide a complete and clear picture of students' strengths and challenges. McTighe (2008) referred to this system as creating a "photo album" of a student rather than simply taking a "snapshot." In this approach, mul-tiple sources of evidence are gathered over time, with each type serving a particular purpose. Figure 2.2 provides a visual representation of this balanced assessment system from a systems perspective. Terms may carry a different connotation at a classroom level.

As can be seen, summative assessments are large-scale and are used to determine how groups of students, school districts, and the state are progressing. They inform curriculum decisions and determine Adequate Yearly Progress (AYP). Examples of summative assessments include state testing systems and the National Assessment of Educational Progress (NAEP). Benchmark assessments, such as district common assessments, help determine to what extent students are progressing and how well a program is working. Formative assessments are ongoing and are admin-istered on a daily basis in the classroom. They are used to consider what learning comes next for students and to make timely adjustments in instruction. Formative assessments should include authentic perfor-mance tasks as well as other types of assessments, such as tests, quizzes, journals, presentations, and so on (Wiggins, 1998).

Continuous review of student progress draws on a balanced assess-ment system as a framework for constant inquiry to determine (a) what students know and can do (screening); (b) how students are responding to differentiated, core instruction (ongoing assessment); and (c) how stu-dents are responding to interventions (progress monitoring).

Screening precedes instruction and is critical to making decisions about appropriate learning opportunities for students. It may be sum-mative (e.g., standardized achievement tests), benchmark (e.g., com-mon assessments), or formative (e.g., spelling pretests or KWL charts). The purpose of screening is to assess what students already know and understand and what they can already do. This information guides deci-sions about how to differentiate the core curriculum. Teachers are able to determine how they might scaffold learning opportunities to provide

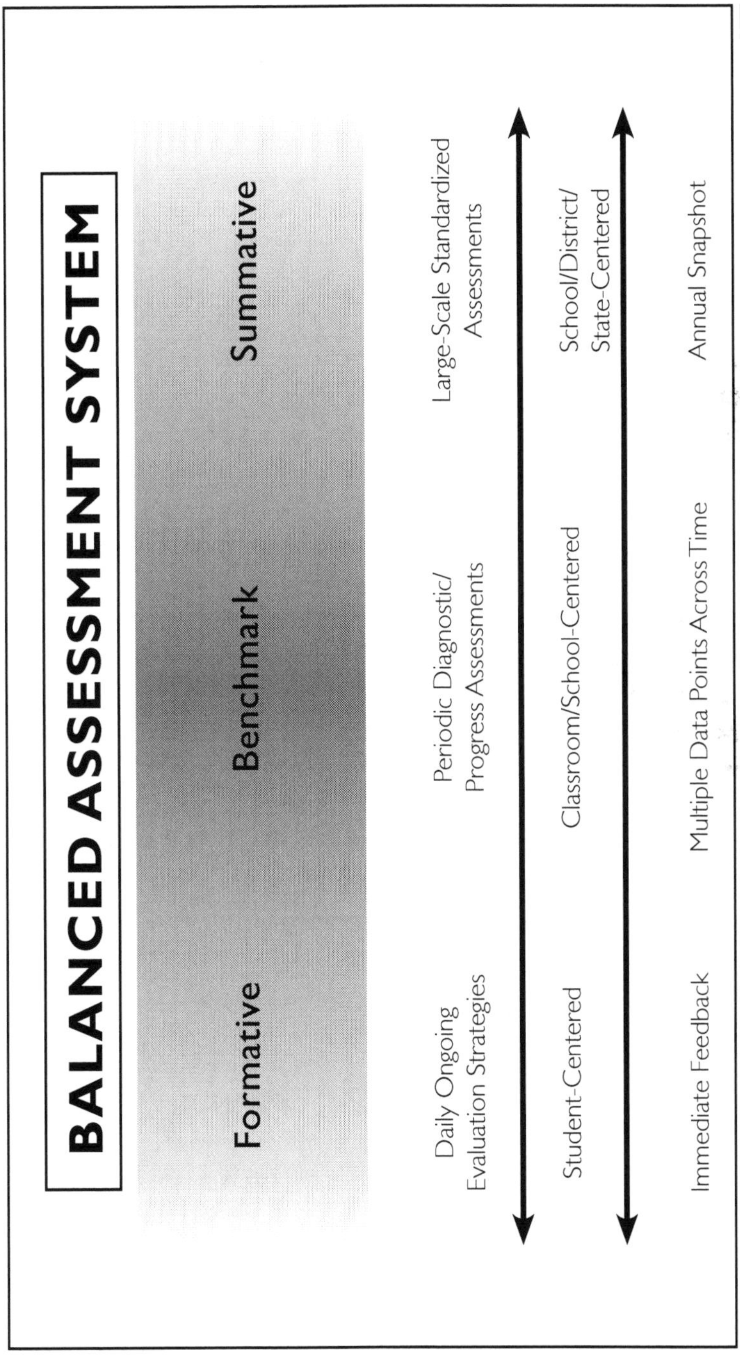

BALANCED ASSESSMENT SYSTEM

Formative	Benchmark	Summative
Daily Ongoing Evaluation Strategies	Periodic Diagnostic/ Progress Assessments	Large-Scale Standardized Assessments
Student-Centered	Classroom/School-Centered	School/District/ State-Centered
Immediate Feedback	Multiple Data Points Across Time	Annual Snapshot

Figure 2.2. Wisconsin DPI balanced assessment system.

struggling students support to be successful or to provide advanced students additional challenge.

Ongoing assessment is most commonly formative. Teachers frequently use different methods to determine the effectiveness of the differentiation they planned. They may use strategies such as thumbs-up-thumbs-down, quizzes, or oral summaries to ascertain whether students are learning. If students are responding to the strategy being used, it is continued. If students are not responding to the strategy, teachers make adjustments.

Progress monitoring is aimed at students who require interventions beyond the core curriculum, whether it is additional support for struggling students or additional challenge for high-ability students. It's important to set individual student targets, to outline instructional strategies, and to closely watch student progress. Daily, formative assessments are used to determine whether students are responding to the intervention and whether anticipated progress is being made. Benchmark, diagnostic assessments (e.g., DIBELS and running records) also can add to the information about student progress. Adjustments to instruction and changes in interventions are made as warranted.

Collaboration. Collaboration is key to making these instructional decisions, as emphasized in Chapter 1. The Wisconsin DPI believes that collaboration is the third component of a successful RtI system. It is important that all staff members have a shared sense of responsibility to increase academic and behavioral growth for every student and a shared sense of accountability for student achievement. The literature makes a strong connection between collaboration and high-quality instruction for all students, a relationship that Wisconsin's RtI framework emphasizes. These collaborative efforts have a positive impact on student achievement (Fullan & Hargreaves, 1991; Zehr, 2006). The literature also suggests that collaboration is an essential element of school change (Gajda & Koliba, 2008). Because RtI represents a systems change, this finding is important. In these times of budget challenges, collaborative approaches can maximize staffing and community resources to support all students.

In Wisconsin's RtI model, teams of educators collaborate using student assessment data to plan and monitor academic and behavioral instruction and intervention. Parents and community partners are also involved in planning decisions and in supporting students. Many schools in the state have a formal collaborative decision-making team. It's important that the composition of this group is fluid, based on the academic and behavioral needs of the students. In one instance, the team might consist of the classroom teacher, the gifted and talented coordinator, the parents, and the school counselor. In another instance, it might consist of the classroom teacher, the special education teacher, the principal, the parents, and a mentor from the local Big Brothers-Big Sisters agency. In yet another instance, the team might consist of the classroom teacher and the reading teacher. Collaboration can also occur on an informal basis, such as when two classroom teachers discuss the needs of a student that they both have.

In Wisconsin, the question asked is, "What systems can be put in place so schools are responsive to all learners?" The Wisconsin DPI believes that the answer lies in Response to Intervention. RtI is a PK–12 initiative for high-quality instruction, continuous review of student progress using a balanced assessment system, and collaboration that has applications for all education: general education, special education, English language learner education, and gifted education. Wisconsin's RtI Roadmap, found in Figure 2.3, visually represents this commitment.

Local Wisconsin RtI models. As previously mentioned, local school districts in Wisconsin make many decisions about curriculum. For this reason, there is no state-prescribed model for RtI or for gifted education—local school districts have developed a variety of models for incorporating gifted education into an RtI system. In this way, they are able to connect local initiatives and maximize local resources. Although the models may be somewhat different, they all include the three main elements of Wisconsin's RtI framework. All provide high-quality instruction that includes increasing intensities of interventions to meet the behavior and academic needs of students. All use multiple forms of data and progress monitoring to make decisions about learning opportunities for students. Finally, all use collaborative problem-solving models to make decisions about students. Let's take a look at three local examples.

Elkhorn Area School District. The Elkhorn Area School District illustrates its problem-solving process using the flowchart found in Figure 2.4. Steps for making decisions about students whose needs go beyond the core curriculum are clearly included, as they are in the Wisconsin RtI Roadmap. What is not articulated in this flowchart, but is explained in accompanying documents, is that the universal assessment relies on preassessment of the targeted skills. This practice is highlighted in other sections of this book. The "Reassess" step in Elkhorn's flowchart represents progress monitoring. In addition to analyzing the data, staff are coached to consider the following questions: Are the tools we used the right tools? What do we need to change? Were we consistent in applying the intervention? What could have affected the child's progress? Do we need to increase the interventions in frequency, duration, or intensity? Do we need more intense interventions?

Ripon Area School District. The Ripon Area School District depicts its RtI system using the common three-tiered graphic (see Figure 2.5). Of special note in this model are the four guiding questions that the school district has used as a focal point for several years (DuFour, DuFour, Eaker, & Many, 2006). These adapted questions are likely familiar: (a) What is it we want our students to learn? (b) How will we know that our students have learned it? (c) What will we do when our students haven't learned it? and (d) What will we do when our students have learned it? Most significant to students with gifts and talents is the fourth question, which could be further adapted to read, "What will we do when students have learned or *already know it*?"

Ripon leadership laid the foundation for RtI using DuFour et al.'s (2006) work so that educators in the district could make connections. In other words, they used a districtwide initiative that was familiar to all staff as a bridge to the less-familiar RtI system. After a year of implementing RtI using this model, Ripon had identified more students with needs beyond the core curriculum in more areas than they did using their previous methods.

Janesville School District. The Janesville School District took the formerly used Wisconsin Pyramid Model for Gifted Education, laid it on its side, and then connected its base to the base of the three-tiered RtI pyramid. The result is a diamond that represents RtI for all students (see Figure 2.6). The school district reinforces appropriate differentiation of the universal high-quality, standards-based curriculum as the initial intervention. The graphic also emphasizes that interventions for students

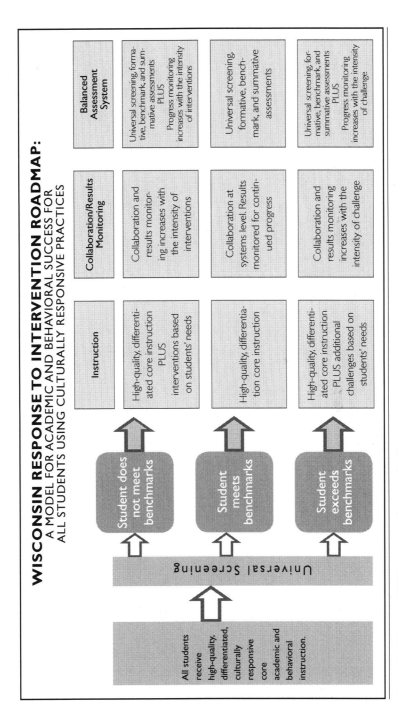

WISCONSIN RESPONSE TO INTERVENTION ROADMAP:
A MODEL FOR ACADEMIC AND BEHAVIORAL SUCCESS FOR
ALL STUDENTS USING CULTURALLY RESPONSIVE PRACTICES

Figure 2.3. Wisconsin DPI Response to Intervention Roadmap.

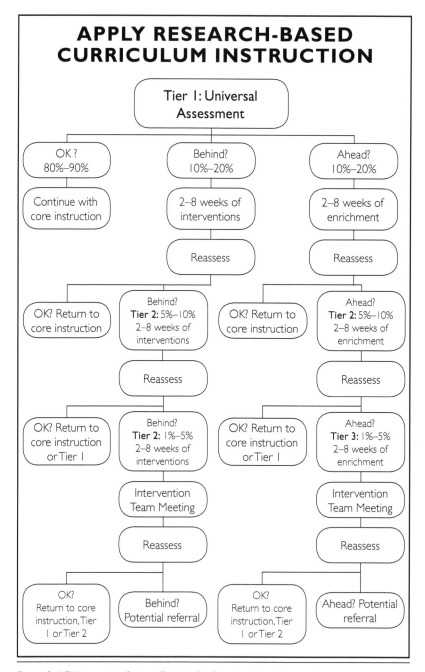

APPLY RESEARCH-BASED CURRICULUM INSTRUCTION

Tier 1: Universal Assessment

| OK ?
80%–90% | Behind?
10%–20% | Ahead?
10%–20% |

Continue with core instruction | 2–8 weeks of interventions | 2–8 weeks of enrichment

Reassess | Reassess

OK? Return to core instruction | Behind?
Tier 2: 5%–10%
2–8 weeks of interventions | OK? Return to core instruction | Ahead?
Tier 2: 5%–10%
2–8 weeks of enrichment

Reassess | Reassess

OK? Return to core instruction or Tier 1 | Behind?
Tier 2: 1%–5%
2–8 weeks of interventions | OK? Return to core instruction or Tier 1 | Ahead?
Tier 3: 1%–5%
2–8 weeks of enrichment

Intervention Team Meeting | Intervention Team Meeting

Reassess | Reassess

OK?
Return to core instruction, Tier 1 or Tier 2 | Behind?
Potential referral | OK?
Return to core instruction, Tier 1 or Tier 2 | Ahead? Potential referral

Figure 2.4. Elkhorn Area School District RtI flowchart for interventions.

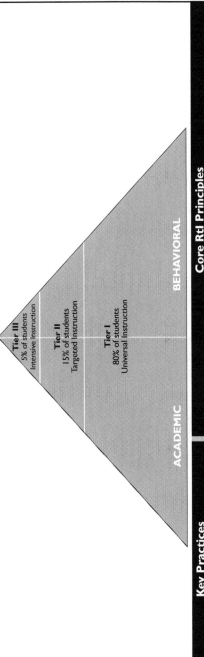

RESPONSE TO INTERVENTION/INSTRUCTION/INSTRUCTION = RTI
RIPON AREA SCHOOL DISTRICT

RtI is the practice of providing high-quality instruction and interventions matched to students' needs, monitoring progress frequently to adjust instruction or goals, and applying student response data to important educational decisions.

Tier III
5% of students
Intensive instruction

Tier II
15% of students
Targeted instruction

Tier I
80% of students
Universal instruction

ACADEMIC | BEHAVIORAL

Key Practices

⟳ RtI is primarily a general education initiative designed to address the needs of all learners.

⟳ RtI is based on a problem-solving model that uses data to inform decision-making.

⟳ RtI interventions are systematically applied and derived from research-based practices.

⟳ RtI is highly dependent on progress monitoring and data collection.

Core RtI Principles

1. RtI supports students' needs by engaging educators in:
   • high-quality instructional practice,
   • continuous review of student progress, and
   • collaboration.

2. RtI is for ALL learners and ALL educators.

3. RtI is required by federal law in NCLB and IDEA.

4. RtI is linked to the Ripon Guiding Questions (DuFour):
   • What is it we want our students to learn?
   • How will we know that our students have learned it?
   • What will we do when our students haven't learned it?
   • What will we do when our students have learned it?

5. RtI applies to both academics and behavior.

Figure 2.5. Ripon Area School District RtI framework.

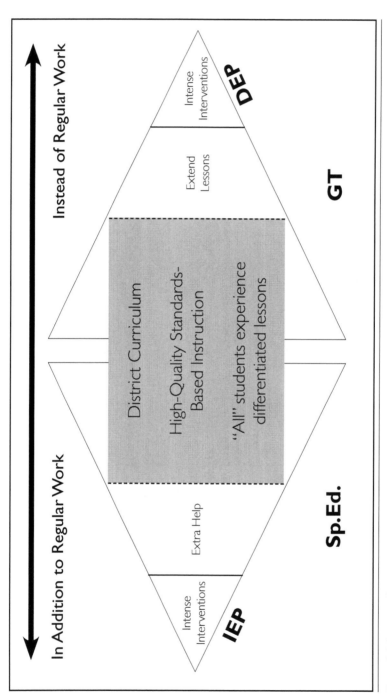

Figure 2.6. Janesville School District RtI model.

with gifts and talents should include tasks that are *instead of* other work rather than *in addition* to it. The school district utilizes a Differentiated Education Plan (DEP) for students who require Tier 3 interventions.

These three examples from local Wisconsin school districts demonstrate that an RtI system can address the needs of students with gifts and talents. They provide proof that this can be accomplished using a variety of models that are developed to reinforce local initiatives and maximize local resources.

COLORADO

The Colorado Department of Education also includes gifted in its definition of RtI: "Response to Intervention is a framework that promotes a well-integrated system connecting general, compensatory, gifted, and special education in providing high quality, standards-based instruction and intervention that is matched to students' academic, social-emotional, and behavioral needs" (Colorado Department of Education, n.d.a., para. 1). In a document entitled, "Response to Intervention—Gifted Education Thinking Points" (Colorado Department of Education, 2006), Colorado articulated the rationale for including students with gifts and talents in its model. The framework incorporates interventions for students with areas of strength and for gifted students who also have an identified disability. The state of Colorado stresses that many aspects of education—compensatory education, special education, and gifted education—can be operated as a "seamless, unified system" (Colorado Department of Education, n.d.b., Slide 52).

Colorado depicted RtI in three tiers (Colorado Department of Education, n.d.a.; see Figure 2.7 and Chapter 4). The Universal Tier uses research-based strategies that are systematic, explicit, and differentiated. The Targeted Tier incorporates small-group and individual instruction that takes into account educational needs such as giftedness. The Intensive Tier provides instruction designed to meet the unique needs of learners at this level. Colorado's model pyramid shows no lines between the tiers to emphasize the fluidity between them. It also shows a problem-solving "flywheel" in the center of the pyramid to represent how decisions are made regarding intensity and the types of interventions needed by stu-

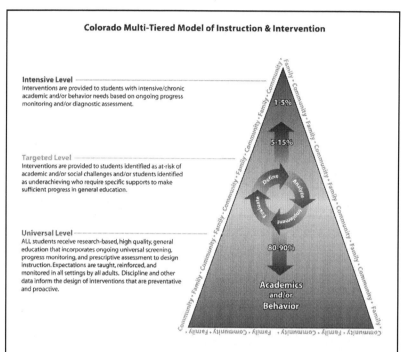

The Colorado RtI Framework has evolved as we learn from implementation. There are no lines separating the tiers because we know that movement between tiers should be fluid; there are no "hoops" for children to jump through in order to receive more or less intensive interventions. The "flywheel" of the multitiered model is the problem-solving process. This process is how decisions are made regarding intensity and type of intervention students need. Our RtI framework is surrounded by "Family and Community" to illustrate the understanding that the education of the child goes beyond the walls of our schools into the homes and communities of our students and to emphasize the importance of partnerships with family and community to support student success.

Figure 2.7. Colorado multitiered model of instruction and intervention.

dents. In addition, the words "Family" and "Community" surround the pyramid to represent the importance of partnerships outside the walls of the school.

OHIO

The Ohio Department of Education (ODE) has developed a

TABLE 2.1
OHIO COMPREHENSIVE SYSTEM
OF LEARNING SUPPORTS

Intervention/ Tier	Academic Systems	Behavioral Systems
Foundation or schoolwide interventions	• Differentiated instruction • Schoolwide enrichment • Metacognitive strategies instruction • Postsecondary enrollment • Curriculum compacting • Advanced educational options • Learning strategies instruction • Student-led conferencing	• Schoolwide counseling • Respecting differences • Leadership training • Teambuilding • Building self-awareness • Learning styles • Futures planning • Cooperative learning • Metacognitive strategies
Early targeted instructional and support interventions	• Acceleration • Mentorships • Independent study • Distance learning coursework • Advanced Placement • Early graduation	• Counseling—Small group • Social skills training • Leadership training
Intensive interventions	• Radical acceleration	• Counseling—Intensive

Comprehensive System of Learning Supports that includes students with gifts and talents (ODE, 2007a; see Table 2.1). An important feature of Ohio's model is the inclusion of interventions for students who show strengths at an advanced grade level and require more accelerated strategies. At Tier 1, "Foundation" or "Schoolwide Interventions," instructional and support systems for all students are provided. At this intervention level, strategies such as advanced educational options, curriculum compacting, and postsecondary enrollment, which may benefit a system's advanced learners, are suggested. At Tier 2, "Early Targeted Instructional and Support Interventions," students with gifts and talents are afforded opportunities such as early graduation, Advanced Placement (AP), and acceleration. Tier 3, "Intensive Interventions," provides support for students with extensive needs. School- and community-based resources, such as afterschool programs and counseling, are made available to enhance the school-family-community partnerships along with radical acceleration options for the very highest level students. Appropriate interventions are offered for twice-exceptional students at each level (ODE, 2007b, p. 81).

UTAH

Utah presents a Four-Tier Model for Gifted and Talented Instruction reflective of RtI to provide quality instruction for students from kindergarten through high school (Utah State Office of Education, n.d.). Tier 1 provides challenging instruction, and differentiates content, process, and products for all students. Emphasis is placed on self-directed learning, which might include flexible instructional grouping, open-ended assignments, and enrichment such as guest speakers and field trips. Tier 2 allows for exploration in areas of strengths and interests through individual and small-group work, and is beyond the required core curriculum for many students. More complex knowledge is emphasized, such as problem-based learning (PBL), future studies, debates, and competitions. Also included is exposure to inquiry experiences, focused enrichment, contracting, and compacting. Tier 3 offers specialized classes, independent study, and specialized programs provided by the school or by outside agencies for some students. More sophisticated instruction is offered by individuals trained to work with students with gifts and talents and/or trained to teach pull-out programming, cluster classrooms, self-contained gifted and talented classrooms, or honors, concurrent enrollment, AP, or International Baccalaureate (IB) classes. Tier 4 is designed for the few students whose needs are best met using strategies such as radical acceleration, early entrance to high school or college, individual advisement, magnet programs, mentorships, and internships.

SUMMARY

These examples of state and local RtI models demonstrate that the needs of students with gifts and talents can be incorporated explicitly and systematically into a comprehensive educational framework. Originally conceptualized as an early identification system for struggling students,

Response to Intervention holds promise for supporting the academic and behavioral success of all students, including those whose needs go beyond the core curriculum. The state models highlighted in this chapter reveal the possibilities for using RtI as a way to address student abilities as well as disabilities; they are a way to not only address student difficulties but also to nurture student strengths. RtI has the power and promise to transform the nature of the educational system for all students.

REFERENCES

Colorado Department of Education. (2006). *Response to intervention—Gifted education thinking points.* Retrieved from http://www.cde.state.co.us/cdesped/download/pdf/slThinkingPoints_RtIGT.pdf

Colorado Department of Education. (n.d.a.). *Learn about RtI.* Retrieved from http://www.cde.state.co.us/RtI/LearnAboutRtI.htm

Colorado Department of Education. (n.d.b.). *Response to intervention: A framework for educational reform.* Retrieved from http://www.cde.state.co.us/RtI/downloads/PowerPoint/LeadershipTraining.ppt

Danielson, C. (2007). *Enhancing professional practice: A framework for teaching.* Alexandria, VA: Association for Supervision and Curriculum Development.

DuFour, R., DuFour, R., Eaker, R., & Many, T. (2006). *Learning by doing: A handbook for professional learning communities at work.* Bloomington, IN: Solution Tree.

Fullan, M. G., & Hargreaves, A. (1991). *What's worth fighting for: Working together for your school.* Andover, MA: The Regional Laboratory for Educational Improvement of the Northeast and Islands.

Gajda, R., & Koliba, C. J. (2008). Evaluating and improving the quality of teacher collaboration: A field-tested framework for secondary school leaders. *NASSP Bulletin, 92,* 133–153.

McTighe, J. (2008, October). *Connecting content and kids: Integrating differentiation and understanding by design.* Workshop presented at the Wisconsin Association for Supervision and Curriculum Development Conference, Appleton, WI.

Ohio Department of Education. (2007a). *A comprehensive system of learning supports guidelines.* Retrieved from http://www.edresourcesohio.org

Ohio Department of Education. (2007b). *Twice exceptional guide: Preparing Ohio schools to close the achievement gap for gifted students with disabilities.* Retrieved from http://www.edresourcesohio.org

Tomlinson, C. A. (2005). Quality curriculum and instruction for highly able students. *Theory Into Practice, 44,* 160–166.

Utah State Office of Education. (n.d.). *Utah gifted and talented hand-*

book. Retrieved from http://www.schools.utah.gov/curr/gift_talent/default.htm

Wiggins, G. (1998). *Educative assessment: Designing assessments to inform and improve student performance*. Hoboken, NJ: Jossey-Bass.

Zehr, M. A. (2006). Team teaching helps close language gap. *Education Week, 26*(14), 26–29.

CHAPTER 3

Remembering the Importance of Potential: Tiers 1 and 2

Mary Ruth Coleman and Sneha Shah-Coltrane

Diversity and Developing Gifts and Talents: A National Call to Action (The Association for the Gifted [TAG], 2009) calls on educators to address issues of race, culture, ethnicity, language, class, gender, and sexual orientation as they work to provide equity and excellence for all students. This call to action, setting diversity as a key agenda for the field of gifted education, is critical to ensure that all children have access to the highest quality learning opportunities to nurture and respond to their potential (Baldwin, 2007; Ford, 2007; Hertzog, 2005). In spite of years of awareness of the disproportionately low representation of children of cultural and ethnic diversity and poverty receiving gifted education services, this underrepresentation continues in many schools (Ford & Grantham, 2003; Henfield, Washington, & Owens, 2010; National Research Council, 2002). Children who do not have access to these services are educationally vulnerable and will struggle to reach their potential (Coleman & Shah-Coltrane, 2010a). Gaining access to high-quality, challenging, and enriching learning environments depends on the school the student attended, which is largely dependent on where the student lives. In other words, address drives access (Coleman, Shah-Coltrane, Harradine, & Timmons, 2007).

WHY IS NURTURING POTENTIAL SO IMPORTANT?

Blanchett, Klinger, and Harry's (2009) discussion of the convergence of race, culture, language, and disability has bearing as educators reflect on children with high potential. Blanchett and her colleagues remind us that while 70% of African American students, 71% of Hispanic students, and 23% of White students live in poverty, 47% of these African American students, 51% of these Hispanic students, and 5% of these White students also attend high-poverty schools. Thus, students of color are much more likely both to live in poverty *and* to attend schools where the majority of the children are also faced with poverty. This concentration of children from cultural and ethnically diverse and poverty backgrounds is alarming because the quality of resources and learning opportunities is often lower in these schools, and so children face a type of double jeopardy (Ford, 2007). When children do not have access to high-quality, challenging, and enriching learning opportunities, they are educationally vulnerable and will struggle to reach their potential (Coleman & Shah-Coltrane, 2010a).

Potential has been part of our conceptualization of giftedness for many years. It is included in the Marland Report's (1972) and the National Commission on Excellence in Education's (1983) definitions of giftedness. Potential is amazing but fragile. As educators know, an acorn has the potential to become an oak tree; however, it also has the potential to become squirrel food. Potential can be either manifest or latent and in all cases potential does better when it is recognized and nurtured. Perhaps the most important question facing educators as a field is: How can we create high-quality, challenging, and enriching learning opportunities that allow teachers to nurture, recognize, and respond to *all* children's potential?

HISTORY OF NURTURING POTENTIAL WITHIN GIFTED EDUCATION

Educators have known for years that a child's potential can be fluid and that the environment that is provided for learning will influence how this potential unfolds (Gallagher & Gallagher, 1994; Witty, 1951). Bristow, Craig, Hallock, and Laycock (1951), in Paul Witty's seminal book *The Gifted Child*, offered this advice about the identification process for gifted children:

> Recognition of the fact that giftedness may be found anywhere, that it manifests itself in many forms, and is only a potentiality which may be slow in developing or completely inhibited has led in recent years to the definition of what may be called the best cultural medium for giftedness. This cultural medium is an environment which makes it possible for each child to reach the highest level of learning and accomplishment of which he is capable at each stage of his development. (p. 12)

Almost 60 years later, the field continues to focus on creating environments that both nurture and respond to the child's potential.

Don Treffinger proposed a multitiered model for services to address four levels of needs for children: All, Many, Some, and Few. His approach provides scaffolded support to address students' strengths and needs (Coleman & Harrison, 1997):

- *All* children need and deserve a challenging and enriched learning environment.
- *Many* children have periodic needs that go beyond this (e.g., when they develop a strong interest in an area of study or master a given concept more rapidly).
- *Some* children have sustainable needs for differentiation within a content area (e.g., a child with a strength in math may need advanced and accelerated instruction).
- *Few* children will have needs that go well beyond those of others

and will need an individualized education plan (e.g., a student whose strengths across the curriculum require grade acceleration or access to curriculum and instruction at a significantly higher level).

This framework is very much like the Response to Intervention approach. Several other approaches and models within gifted education also address nurturing potential and providing appropriate responses to support children's success.

The Schoolwide Enrichment Model (Renzulli & Reis, 2002) addresses all children's need for enrichment (Type I experiences) and access to higher level thinking/process skills (Type II support). The use of curriculum compacting, to preassess the students' learning and match instruction, a key part of the schoolwide enrichment approach, is similar to the progress monitoring used in RtI. Betts's (Betts & Kercher, 1999) Autonomous Learner Model provides support for developing self-awareness and nurturing self-directed learning. The philosophy of this model is that as learners' needs are met, they will become increasingly more autonomous and self-directed with the ability to set and carry out their own goals for learning.

In addition to models that support the nurturing of all learners, gifted education has been on the vanguard of developing curriculum and instruction approaches that address each child's strengths. VanTassel-Baska (VanTassel-Baska & Little, 2011) has developed curriculum that nurtures and responds to children's learning strengths; Shelagh Gallagher has focused on the use of problem-based learning (PBL) to nurture potential (Gallagher & Gallagher, 1994); and Tomlinson (1999) has focused on curriculum differentiation to respond to the needs of all learners. These models and curriculum/instructional approaches address the need to nurture potential and to respond to the strengths of each child, while addressing those with high ability as well. RtI, with a strong Tier 1 and 2, can also focus on nurturing and responding to potential.

RTI AS AN APPROACH TO NURTURING POTENTIAL

The RtI approach with its multitiered supports and services provides a framework that requires collaboration (Fuchs & Fuchs, 2006; Kirk, Gallagher, Coleman, & Anastasiow, 2009). The aim of this collaboration is to provide an optimal learning environment with the necessary level of support for each child to succeed (Coleman, Roth, & West, 2009). RtI, as a comprehensive school reform, addresses all children and offers a systemic approach to providing supports and enhancements to match the strengths and needs of each child (Kirk et al., 2009). Thus, when a child needs additional time, direct instruction, or practice for learning, these strategies are provided. Likewise, if a child needs additional challenge, enrichment, or independence in learning, these strategies are provided.

The foundation of this framework, Tier 1, is the provision of a high-quality learning environment with appropriately differentiated curriculum to support learning for all children. Through frequent progress monitoring, teachers can recognize when a child's needs go beyond the level of support or enhancement provided in Tier 1, and additional modifications can be made with interventions at Tier 2. With a strong Tier 1, teachers are able to provide a nurturing environment for all of their students to optimally learn; with progress monitoring they can recognize their students' strengths and needs and can respond with additional supports or enhancements at Tier 2. This iterative process of nurturing all children, recognizing strengths and needs that go beyond the standard curriculum and instruction, and responding to these needs is built into the data-driven collaborative framework of RtI. Another gifted educational approach that fits within the RtI framework is specifically designed to nurture the potential of young children of cultural diversity, poverty, and linguistic diversity: U-STARS~PLUS.

NURTURING POTENTIAL IN YOUNG CHILDREN: U-STARS~PLUS

U-STARS~PLUS (Using Science, Talents, and Abilities to Recognize Students~Promoting Learning for Underrepresented Students) focuses on the early nurturing, recognition, and response to children with outstanding potential in the early years of schooling. Early intervention to bring out the best in young children depends on intentionally creating classroom and school environments that nurture potential. By intentionally bringing out the best in students, educators are able to maximize outstanding potential, create an achievement-orientation to schooling, and ensure that children's needs are met. The U-STARS~PLUS approach is centered in the K–3 regular education classroom and serves all students with more intense interventions provided for children who show additional needs. With the focus on general education, supports can be offered prior to formal identification. Nurturing potential in young learners is important because formal gifted identification is often delayed until the later years of elementary school (grades 2–3). By this time, some children will have already lost ground and will be even more likely to be overlooked.

U-STARS~PLUS is designed to help schools address the needs of children with high potential from educationally vulnerable populations, which include children from economically disadvantaged and/or culturally/linguistically diverse families and children with disabilities. Children's educational success may be jeopardized when a variety of factors combine to make school more challenging. These factors may include environmental risks, familial stressors, and individual school readiness gaps. Educationally vulnerable children, however, face their greatest risk when schools are not designed to meet their needs (Shah-Coltrane & Coleman, 2010). The core beliefs that form the foundation for U-STARS~PLUS are:

1. All children deserve access to challenging and enriching learning opportunities.
2. All children deserve to be viewed as "at potential" versus "at risk."

3. Science is a naturally interesting and engaging subject that capti-vates young children's learning.
4. Family involvement is key to sustained support for children.
5. The support we provide to a child's teacher is critical to the suc-cess of the child (Coleman & Shah-Coltrane, 2010a).

The heart of the U-STARS~PLUS approach is to nurture, rec-ognize, and respond to the strengths of young children. Five primary U-STARS~PLUS components, shown in Figure 3.1, are High-End Learning Opportunities, Teachers' Systematic Observations (centered around the Teacher's Observation of Potential in Students [TOPS] form; Coleman, Shah-Coltrane, & Harrison, 2010a, 2010b), Hands-On/ Inquiry-Based Science, Family and School Partnerships, and Infrastructure Building for Systemic Change. When taken together, they synergize to have the greatest impact for children to maximize their potential.

U-STARS~PLUS classroom support materials, Science & Literature Connections (Coleman & Shah-Coltrane, 2010c) and Family Science Packets (Coleman & Shah-Coltrane, 2010a), are designed to help teach-ers create a high-end learning environment. The materials incorporate basic principles of differentiated instruction in concrete ways so that the teacher can provide meaningfully enriched and challenging science content while simultaneously developing his or her own ability to dif-ferentiate lessons. Science & Literature Connections (Coleman & Shah-Coltrane, 2010c) specifically focuses integrating science with literature through questions that elicit higher levels of thinking from students. The Family Science Packets (Coleman & Shah-Coltrane, 2010a) are designed to complement and extend the school's science curriculum and instruction while modeling differentiation and hands-on/inquiry-based approaches to learning. All of the U-STARS~PLUS science materials are based on the National Science Education Standards (National Research Council, 1996) and are designed to align with and extend the school's science curriculum.

When children are engaged in learning, using active, inquiry-based, enriched materials within a high-end learning environment, educators are able to see their strengths if they are looking for them. This high-

U-STARS~PLUS

Using Science, Talents, and Abilities to Recognize Students ~ Promoting Learning for Underrepresented Students

TEACHERS' SYSTEMATIC OBSERVATIONS

☆ "At potential" versus "at risk" mindset

☆ Teacher's Observation of Potential in Students (TOPS), a teacher tool to recognize students with outstanding potential from underserved populations

☆ Building a body of evidence, using informal and formal measures over time

HANDS-ON/INQUIRY-BASED SCIENCE

☆ Promotes thinking, achievement, and language development

☆ Captivates students' interest through real-world setting and content integration

☆ Focuses on exploration and problem solving; not solely based on traditional expository methods/verbal skills

FAMILY and SCHOOL PARTNERSHIPS

☆ Family involvement programs

☆ Effective parent conferences and communication

☆ Family Science Packets

☆ Cultural understanding (impact of poverty, diversity, and social/emotional needs)

HIGH-END LEARNING OPPORTUNITIES

☆ Curriculum differentiation
  → curriculum compacting
  → tiered activities
  → learning centers/stations
  → independent studies/group projects
  → questioning/higher order thinking skills

☆ Dynamic assessment to inform classroom instruction

☆ Flexible grouping

☆ Classroom support materials:
  → Science and Literature Connections
  → Family Science Packets

INFRASTRUCTURE BUILDING for SYSTEMIC CHANGE

☆ Capacity building of leadership and teachers (i.e., professional development and policy)

☆ Fidelity of implementation (district, school, classroom)

☆ Accountability (district, school, classroom, child)

NURTURE — RECOGNIZE — RESPOND

Figure 3.1. U-STARS~PLUS components.

end learning environment provides the ideal context for a teacher to use systematic observations so that a student's potential can be recognized.

Systematic observation involves a shift in perspective, changing how educators view children who come from educationally vulnerable populations (i.e., children from culturally/linguistically diverse and/or economically disadvantaged families, and children with disabilities). Educators have traditionally viewed these children as "at risk," and this view has promoted interventions that focus on minimizing risk and remediating deficits. The U-STARS~PLUS approach takes an "at potential" view of children, focusing on maximizing children's potential by creating environments that respond to their strengths.

Using the TOPS form (Coleman et al., 2010a; see Figure 3.2) helps teachers recognize children (ages 5–9) who have outstanding potential and who *may* be gifted. In the development of the TOPS, specific attention was given to the recognition of educationally vulnerable children whose potential has historically been overlooked.

The focus on science is also central to U-STARS~PLUS because science is the ideal platform to nurture, recognize, and respond to outstanding potential in young children (Shah-Coltrane & Coleman, 2005). Science is especially helpful when educators are looking for potential in children who will not be able to show them their strengths through language alone (Amaral, Garrison, & Klentschy, 2002; Carlson, 2000; Simich-Dudgeon & Egbert, 2000). Science that is inquiry-based and hands-on allows children to learn about their world with an emphasis on exploration and problem solving (Basile, 1999; Donnellan & Roberts, 1985). Active learning differs from traditional expository methods that are dependent upon reading and writing. When children are "doing" science, they have natural and authentic reasons to talk, read, write, and engage in mathematical thinking (Nyberg & McCloskey, 2008). In science, students have a chance to demonstrate their thinking and reasoning even before they have the words to fully express their understandings; thus, the words and language can be developed (Simich-Dudgeon & Egbert, 2000).

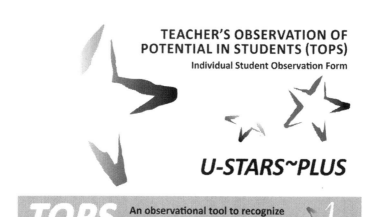

TEACHER'S OBSERVATION OF POTENTIAL IN STUDENTS (TOPS)

Individual Student Observation Form

U-STARS~PLUS

TOPS An observational tool to recognize outstanding potential in children.

Purpose

The Teacher's Observation of Potential in Students (TOPS) is a tool to help you recognize children (ages 5-9) with outstanding potential who may be gifted. The TOPS is designed to be the teacher observation component of a comprehensive approach to recognizing students with outstanding potential. This tool should complement other sources of information. The TOPS is organized around nine domains: (1) Learns Easily, (2) Shows Advanced Skills, (3) Displays Curiosity & Creativity, (4) Has Strong Interests, (5) Shows Advanced Reasoning & Problem Solving, (6) Displays Spatial Abilities, (7) Shows Motivation, (8) Shows Social Perceptiveness, and (9) Displays Leadership. Examples of behaviors that can be used as indicators of potential are given for each domain. These behaviors capture both "teacher pleasing" and "non-teacher pleasing" behaviors because bright children are not always "teacher-pleasers". Non-teacher pleasing behaviors can sometimes impede our recognition of students' potential. As you use the Individual TOPS, please remember to observe the child in multiple settings over time to best see her/his potential.

Directions

1. Select a 3-6 week time period to observe the child using the Individual TOPS.
2. Complete the tab on the TOPS folder.
3. When you observe the child's behavior, within a specific domain, write down the date and a short note describing the observation in the box for that domain.
4. Each additional time you observe the child within a specific domain, add a date and note to the box.
5. If you have work samples or materials connected to the observation, collect them in the TOPS folder. This collection will serve as an initial body-of-evidence documenting the child's potential. This body-of-evidence can be used in planning for the child.
6. After your observation period is initially completed, compile and reflect on your observations on the back of the Individual Student TOPS. Continue documenting your observations and classroom responses as needed.

Next Steps

After completing your observations using the Individual TOPS, you will be making decisions about how to follow-up with this child's strengths and needs. In making these decisions you should consider the following:

1. What are this child's major strengths? In which domains does she/he show outstanding potential?
2. How can I better respond to this student's potential? What can I do to meet this child's needs in my classroom?
3. Would additional information help me better understand and plan instruction for this child? If yes, how can I gather this information?
4. Should I nominate this child for possible identification as gifted?

You may wish to contact the child's parents to notify them that you have observed indications that their child may have outstanding potential and to set up a conference. This conference would allow you to get parental input, to share your observations, and to reflect together about how to best meet the needs of the child.

Authors: Mary Ruth Coleman, Sneha Shah-Coltrane, Ann Harrison

previously known as the "Harrison Observation Student Form"

Figure 3.2. Sample TOPS Individual Student Form.

LEARNS EASILY
Is eager to learn.
Has lots of information.
Retains and retrieves information easily.
Carries out complex instructions with ease.
Completes assignments ahead of others (gets A's without effort).
Shows strong memory, quick recall.
Uses complex language & math symbol systems.
Prefers work with more complexity.
Refuses and becomes impatient with tedious and repetitious work.
Appears bored with or rushes through "easy" work.
Corrects the teacher and students in class.
Does not show work, only answers.

SHOWS ADVANCED SKILLS
Reads and comprehends on an advanced level (this may be seen
    in listening comprehension).
Tells or reproduces stories and events with detail.
Has a large vocabulary.
Uses descriptive language, similies, puns.
Makes up songs, stories, and rhymes.
Spends free time absorbed in books (may read when supposed to
    do other things).
Seeks non-fiction as well as fiction.
Generates many writing ideas and products.
Understands advanced mathematical concepts.
Understands the meaning and use of maps, diagrams, and graphs.
Connects and uses mathematical language and skills in meaningful
    real-world ways.
Communicates well with symbols (art, design, music, or dance).
Carries on conversations related to academic topics and within a discipline.
Masters and shows high level thinking in a specific content area.
Manipulates situations for specific purposes.
Challenges teacher to go further in depth and complexity.

DISPLAYS CURIOSITY & CREATIVITY
Questions, explores, experiments.
Asks unusual, provocative questions.
Is curious. Asks how, why, and what if?
Tries to discover the how and why of things.
Enjoys doing things in new ways.
Puts unrelated ideas and materials together in new and different ways.
Offers unique responses.
Has an active imagination (likes to pretend).
Assumes another persona during activities or conversations.
Has trouble distinguishing fact from fiction.
Does not follow or wait for directions (makes own rules).
Refuses to follow rules unless they see "why."
Is seen as "deviant" or non-comformist.
Develops and tells elaborate "stories."

HAS STRONG INTERESTS
Is able to lose self in something of interest.
Demonstrates unusual or advanced interests.
Keeps extensive collections.
Is considered an "expert" in a particular topic (may seem domineering).
Checks books on particular topics.
Chooses to become involved when area of interest is addressed.
Has interest in areas outside typical school curriculum.
Leads discussions back to one topic of interest.
Resist transition moving onto a new topic of study.

Figure 3.2., Continued.

SHOWS ADVANCED REASONING & PROBLEM SOLVING
Is a keen observer (spots details others miss).
Recognizes patterns.
Draws accurate and advanced conclusions based on information.
Designs experiments to test hypotheses (develops logical ways to collect and
    analyze data).
Makes mental connections (transfers learning into other subjects or real
    life situations).
Sees cause and effect relationships. Asks "why?"
Expresses relationships between past and present.
Is aware of problems others do not see.
Devises or adapts strategies to solve problems.
Questions "rote" approaches to problem solving.
Has "out of the box" ways of solving problems ad seeing situations.
Doesn't do well on tests with limited answer choices.
Is argumentative.

DISPLAYS SPATIAL ABILITIES
Has a good sense of direction.
Figures out why and how things work.
Takes objects apart and reassembles with speed and accuracy.
Creates interesting shapes and patterns.
Shows unusual talent in various art forms.
Invents games.
Creates three-dimensional structures.
Has excellent motor planning and coordination.
Needs movement to connect learning to memory.
Prefers hands-on experiences to learn (uses manipulatives/artifacts).
Brings gadgets, toys, etc. to tinker with at school.
Moves around often (keeps hands and body always busy).

SHOWS MOTIVATION
Is a self-starter (requires little direction).
Is persistent in pursuing and completing self-selected tasks.
Is independent (requires little feedback).
Prefers to do things on own ("the quiet child").
Enjoys challenge of new and different.
Prefers interacting with older people.
Converses about mature topics.
Does not follow typical path (moves to the beat of a different drummer).
Questions authority (is considered a "trouble-maker" or instigator).

SHOWS SOCIAL PERCEPTIVENESS
Displays sense of humor (may be "class clown").
Responds to needs of others (is able to see another's point of view).
Enjoys working in groups.
Identifies with individuals in books, history, movies, etc.
Uses skills to resolve conflict.
Reads social situations well and can gain acceptance in most groups.
Displays strong sense of justice (may over-react emotionally).
Is easily distracted by others' needs.
Is over-talkative and social.
Uses humor and sarcasm inappropriately.

DISPLAYS LEADERSHIP
Organizes materials and activities.
Accepts and carries out responsibilities.
Is sought by others (influences others, positively or negatively).
Adapts readily to new situations and changes.
Is a positive and compassionate guide to others.
Prefers adult company.
Is seen as manipulative and strong-willed.
Is seen as "bossy" (wants to be the center of attention).
Dominates others (may not be a good follower).

Figure 3.2., Continued.

INDIVIDUAL TOPS STUDENT PROFILE

Student Demographics:

Name	Birth Date	Gender	Race	ESL/ELL Y or N?	Disability Areas	Low SES Y or N?	Urban/ suburban/ rural

I believe this student shows outstanding potential in the classroom.
Indicate the TOPS domains recognized and describe the student potential and behaviors.

Domain	Check reason why recognized:		Summary of Observation(s); Best Example	Classroom Responses and Teacher Modifications
	Frequency	Intensity		
Learns Easily				
Shows Advanced Skills				
Displays Curiosity and Creativity				
Has Strong Interests				
Shows Advanced Reasoning and Problem Solving				
Displays Spatial Abilities				
Shows Motivation				
Shows Social Perceptiveness				
Displays Leadership				

Overall Teacher Recommendations:

_____

_____

Coleman, M.R., Shah-Cottrane, S., & Harrison, A. (2010). *Teacher's observation of potential in students: Individual student form.* Arlington, VA: Council for Exceptional Children.

Figure 3.2., Continued.

HOW U-STARS~PLUS FITS WITH RTI

Tier 1. U-STARS~PLUS focuses on high-end learning opportunities, hands-on/inquiry-based science, dynamic assessment, and a systematic whole-class-to-individual observation of potential. Creating a high-end learning environment in Tier 1 includes the use of curriculum differentiation, dynamic assessment, flexible grouping, and classroom support materials to enhance learning. By using the TOPS form, the general education classroom teacher ensures that all children are given the support and opportunity to show their best work, without a predetermined decision as to who is "gifted." The TOPS form is a classroom observational tool to guide teachers as they observe their children in multiple settings over time and recognize outstanding potential. U-STARS~PLUS is founded on a key principle that a child's needs are best understood by building a body of evidence that incorporates multiple perspectives of that child. In a classroom environment that intentionally cultivates potential, the TOPS begins with a whole-class observation, ensuring that all children are being observed systematically, and leads to individual observations of children as the need becomes apparent. As teachers utilize the TOPS form, their views of children refocuses from "at risk" to "at potential," and they further modify the curriculum and instruction to respond to the children's needs.

Tier 2. Based on the whole-class observation of students in the general education classroom, guided by the TOPS, students who may need more support are recognized. At this point, an individual TOPS is completed along with work sampling and other classroom assessments to help teachers understand the child's strengths and needs. Based on this evidence, a plan for differentiated curriculum and instruction is developed. Differentiated instruction is primarily delivered in the general education classroom using a variety of strategies, including science as a focused content area. By providing differentiated experiences in science, as well as other areas, children become engaged with learning, problem solve in meaningful ways, and develop literacy skills and content-rich concepts and understandings. Collaboration with gifted education specialists at this level is also helpful. This process is ongoing, and teachers are encouraged to look for students who may need additional enrichment and challenge throughout the year. Families are often included in discussion of the child's strengths at this level of support.

Tier 3. As observation and classroom responses continue, more intense and individualized services are provided to meet the needs of particular children with high-end needs. The individual TOPS is augmented with additional information regarding the child's strengths and needs, and a body of evidence is built to take a closer look at the child. Nomination for formal gifted identification may be considered at this point, and families are included in the decision-making process. The lead for this high level of support may be the gifted education specialist.

Dynamic assessment (progress monitoring). In order for support and services to match student needs, dynamic assessment that informs instruction is crucial. U-STARS~PLUS uses the TOPS as the focus for systematic teacher observation of students to inform classroom instruction. Beginning with the whole-class observation in Tier 1 and moving toward individual observations helps teachers match children's strengths to curricula and instruction early to ensure their success. Teachers use basic differentiation strategies so that as students' needs change, their learning experiences can be adjusted. Curriculum compacting is also used along with assessments designed to document the students' learning needs. These assessment practices help teachers to monitor the progress of the children, documenting each child's mastery of the curriculum so that appropriate next steps can be planned.

Collaboration. Meaningful partnerships with families are critical. Partnerships create the opportunity for educators and families to learn together and work toward creating the most appropriate learning experiences for children. U-STARS~PLUS believes that collaboration, with both school personnel and families of students, is critical to ensuring success for the child. Types of collaboration include the following examples:

- The TOPS is used with input from other school personnel and from family members to provide a more complete understanding of a child's strengths and needs.
- The Family Science Packets (Coleman & Shah-Coltrane, 2010a), which are also translated into Spanish, are take-home "science in a bag" activities for children to complete with their families, extending the partnership further with an academic platform.

- The family involvement programs and events at U-STARS-PLUS schools create invitational opportunities for family participation.
- When educators use the TOPS to document the strengths of their students, they can connect this information to instructional planning to meet students' needs and can share their insights during parent conferences where they focus on a child's strengths. This focus on a child's strengths, combined with the Family Science Packets (Coleman & Shah-Coltrane, 2010a), brings teachers and parents together in a shared positive view of the child's academic potential, which builds trusting relationships between the family and the school personnel.

Collaboration is central to the success of both RtI and to the U-STARS-PLUS approach and true, meaningful collaboration may be the key to actually meeting the needs of our students.

SUMMARY

Gifted education has a long and strong history of supporting the importance of nurturing potential. As a field, professionals have developed models, approaches, and materials to help teachers recognize and respond to children with outstanding potential and high ability. Yet in spite of this, the field has not been able to ensure that the strengths of all children are nurtured; therefore, children who are educationally vulnerable are overlooked. This may be because gifted educators have not yet found a way to truly collaborate with our general and special education partners in supporting emerging abilities by creating an "environment which makes it possible for each child to reach the highest level of learning and accomplishment of which he is capable at each stage of his development" (Bristow et al., 1951, p. 12). Perhaps RtI will provide this opportunity.

REFERENCES

Amaral, O. M., Garrison, L., & Klentschy, M. (2002). Helping English learners increase achievement through inquiry-based science instruction. *Bilingual Research Journal, 26,* 214–239.

Baldwin, A. Y. (2007). The untapped potential for excellence. In J. VanTassel-Baska & T. Stambaugh (Eds.), *Overlooked gems: A national perspective on low-income promising learners* (pp. 23–25). Washington, DC: National Association for Gifted Children.

Basile, C. G. (1999). Collecting data outdoors: Making connections to the real world. *Teaching Children Mathematics, 6*(1), 8–11.

Betts, G. T., & Kercher, J. K. (1999). *Autonomous Learner Model: Optimizing ability.* Greeley, CO: ALPS Publishing.

Blanchett, W. J., Klinger, J. K., & Harry, B. (2009). The intersection of race, culture, language, and disability: Implications for urban education. *Urban Education, 44,* 389–409.

Bristow, W. H., Craig, M. L., Hallock, G. T., & Laycock, S. R. (1951). Identifying gifted children. In P. Witty (Ed.), *The gifted child* (pp. 10–19). Boston, MA: D. C. Heath and Company.

Carlson, C. (2000). Scientific literacy for all: Helping English language learners make sense of academic language. *Science Teacher, 67*(3), 48–52.

Coleman, M. R., & Harrison, A. (1997). *Programming for gifted learners: Developing a system level plan for service delivery.* Chapel Hill: The University of North Carolina.

Coleman, M., Roth, F., & West, T. (2009). *Roadmap to pre-k RTI: Applying response to intervention in preschool settings.* New York, NY: National Center for Learning Disabilities.

Coleman, M. R., & Shah-Coltrane, S. (2010a). *U-STARS~PLUS family science packets.* Arlington, VA: Council for Exceptional Children.

Coleman, M. R., & Shah-Coltrane, S. (2010b). *U-STARS~PLUS professional development kit.* Arlington, VA: Council for Exceptional Children.

Coleman, M. R., & Shah-Coltrane, S. (2010c). *U-STARS~PLUS science & literature connections.* Arlington, VA: Council for Exceptional Children.

Coleman, M. R., Shah-Coltrane, S., Harradine, C., & Timmons, L. A. (2007). Impact of poverty on promising learners, their teachers, and their schools. In J. VanTassel-Baska & T. Stambaugh (Eds.), *Overlooked gems: A national perspective on low-income promising learners* (pp. 59–61). Washington, DC: National Association for Gifted Children.

Coleman, M. R., Shah-Coltrane, S., & Harrison, A. (2010a). *Teacher's observation of potential in students: Individual student form*. Arlington, VA: Council for Exceptional Children.

Coleman, M. R., Shah-Coltrane, S., & Harrison, A. (2010b). *Teacher's observation of potential in students: Whole class form*. Arlington, VA: Council for Exceptional Children.

Donnellan, K., & Roberts, G. (1985). What research says: Activity-based elementary science: A double bonus. *Science and Children, 22*(4), 119–121.

Ford, D. Y. (2007). Diamonds in the rough: Recognizing and meeting the needs of gifted children from low SES backgrounds. In J. VanTassel-Baska & T. Stambaugh (Eds.), *Overlooked gems: A national perspective on low-income promising learners* (pp. 37–41). Washington, DC: National Association for Gifted Children.

Ford, D. Y., & Grantham, T. C. (2003). Providing access for culturally diverse gifted students: From deficit to dynamic thinking. *Theory Into Practice, 42,* 217–225.

Fuchs, L. S., & Fuchs, D. (2006). A framework for building capacity for responsiveness to intervention. *School Psychology Review, 35,* 621–626.

Gallagher, J., & Gallagher, S. (1994). *Teaching the gifted child* (4th ed.). Needham Heights, MA: Paramount.

Henfield, M. S., Washington, A. R., & Owens, D. (2010). To be or not to be gifted: The choice for a new generation. *Gifted Child Today, 32*(2), 17–25.

Hertzog, N. (2005). Equity and access: Creating general education classrooms responsive to potential giftedness. *Journal for the Education of the Gifted, 29,* 213–257.

Kirk, S., Gallagher, J., Coleman, M. R., & Anastasiow, N. (2009).

Educating exceptional children (12th ed.). Boston, MA: Houghton Mifflin.

Marland, S. P., Jr. (1972). *Education of the gifted and talented: Report to the Congress of the United States by the U.S. Commissioner of Education and background papers submitted to the U.S. Office of Education,* 2 vols. Washington, DC: U.S. Government Printing Office. (Government Documents, Y4.L 11/2: G36)

National Commission on Excellence in Education. (1983). *A nation at risk: The imperative for educational reform.* Washington, DC: U.S. Government Printing Office.

National Research Council. (1996). *National science education standards.* Washington, DC: National Academy Press.

National Research Council. (2002). *Minority students in special and gifted education.* Washington, DC: National Academy Press.

Nyberg, L., & McCloskey, S. (2008). Integration with integrity. *Science & Children, 46*(3), 46–49.

Renzulli, J., & Reis, S. (2002). What is school-wide enrichment? How gifted programs relate to school improvement. *Gifted Child Today, 25*(4), 18–25.

Shah-Coltrane, S., & Coleman, M. R. (2005, Fall/Winter). Using science as a vehicle: Search for outstanding potential in underserved populations. *Gifted Education Communicator, 36,* 20–23.

Simich-Dudgeon, C., & Egbert, J. (2000). Science as a second language: Verbal interactive strategies help English language learners develop academic vocabulary. *Science Teacher, 67*(3), 28–32.

The Association for the Gifted. (2009). *Diversity and developing gifts and talents: A national call to action.* Retrieved from http://www.cectag.org

Tomlinson, C. A. (1999). *The differentiated classroom: Responding to the needs of all learners.* Alexandria, VA: Association for Supervision and Curriculum Development.

VanTassel-Baska, J., & Little, C. A. (Eds.). (2011). *Content-based curriculum for high-ability learners* (2nd ed.). Waco, TX: Prufrock Press.

Witty, P. (Ed.). (1951). *The gifted child.* Boston, MA: D. C. Heath and Company.

CHAPTER 4

Addressing the Needs of Students Who Are Twice-Exceptional

Daphne Pereles, Lois Baldwin,
and Stuart Omdal

Many books and articles have been written about a Response to Intervention (RtI) model of service delivery for students who are struggling learners. Little has been written about this model's usefulness as a means of addressing the needs of advanced learners or twice-exceptional learners whose needs may be both remedial and advanced. The National Association of State Directors of Special Education (NASDSE; 2005) defined RtI as the "practice of providing high-quality instruction and interventions matched to student need, monitoring progress frequently to make decisions about changes in instruction or goals and applying child response data to important educational decisions" (p. 3). It further stated that this practice should be used in "general, remedial, and special education" (NASDSE, 2005, p. 3). This statement does not include gifted education. The NASDSE document did not address gifted children, nor did it define "high-quality instruction" as opportunities for acceleration or enrichment.

The Colorado Department of Education (CDE) has a defini-
tion broader in nature and inclusive of all students. It defines RtI as "a
framework that promotes a well-integrated system connecting general,
compensatory, gifted, and special education in providing high quality,
standards-based instruction and intervention that is matched to students'
academic, social–emotional, and behavioral needs." (CDE, 2008, p. 3)
This definition allows for broader application of the foundational principles of an RtI model that truly includes all students, and can be an effective means of addressing the complex needs of twice-exceptional learners.
The Council for Exceptional Children (CEC; 2008), in its "Position
Paper on Response to Intervention," stated that RtI

> shall consider the educational needs of children with gifts and
> talents and their families, particularly related to the identifi-
> cation of children considered to be twice exceptional because
> they have gifts and talents as well as a disability. These advanced
> learners shall be provided access to a challenging and accelerated
> curriculum, while also addressing the unique needs of their dis-
> ability. (p. 2)

This chapter will present an RtI model with a problem-solving/
consultation process as a promising fit for the twice-exceptional student. Theoretical and practical implications for these special students are
described and each element of the problem-solving/consultation process
is discussed through a case study of a gifted student who has both learning and behavioral challenges.

IMPLICATION OF
EDUCATIONAL LABELS

The school population mirrors the population at large with regards
to diversity in language, ethnicity, culture, and ability/disability, and it
has become increasingly difficult to meet the needs of diverse groups
of learners (Cole, 2008). In our effort to categorize and make meaning
of these challenges, identification systems were created, and the practice

of assigning labels to students with special needs has become a vehicle for providing services. These identification systems, although created for all the right reasons—opening doors for funding, raising awareness and understanding, improving communication between professionals and families, and providing a social identity (Lauchlan & Boyle, 2007)—resulted in a disconnected group of isolated programs or "silos" created around student labels. Students began to be assigned to a set "program" based on the label and not always on an identified educational need (NASDSE, 2005). Because of their unique learning needs, twice-exceptional students have never fit neatly into any of the typical programs found in a school system. Their needs have always challenged personnel in this disconnected system of silos and contributed to the students' difficulty of achieving success.

With the advent of RtI, the need to assign labels to students changes. A label is not required for students to receive interventions and support. The responsibility for student success becomes a shared responsibility within a supportive professional environment. Because RtI is structured around the assessed educational needs of students and not the attainment of a label, it is difficult to discuss the framework in regard to a specific, labeled group of students. Applying an older way of systemic thinking onto the RtI model is in a way force-fitting the merger of two paradigms that actually need to be considered in different ways. This step, however, is a necessary step to create a bridge for practitioners to comprehend the application of RtI philosophy and to understand how it differs from current practice. To resolve this dilemma, the term *twice-exceptional student* is being used to denote learners displaying behaviors and characteristics associated with both giftedness and the spectrum of disabilities.

In 1981, Renzulli, Reis, and Smith recommended the labeling of student behaviors rather than labeling students as "gifted." Labeling behaviors helps decision makers develop appropriate educational plans that match individual student strengths, interests, and abilities. The gifted label itself did not help teachers to select appropriate educational programming options for these students. Given the dozens of characteristics and traits associated with giftedness and the personality and environmental factors that affect the development of these characteristics and traits, it is safe to say that those who are identified for gifted education services compose a heterogeneous group. Labeling a group infers homogeneity of the group. Definitions of giftedness and talent and identification processes vary greatly between states—and often in districts within a state. Generalized, stereotypical characteristics assigned to a label cannot reflect the range of characteristics nor can the levels or degrees of those characteristics be adequately captured. These stereotypes, combined with generalized, prescribed instructional strategies, result in an illusion that appropriate instruction is occurring and ignore the range of diversity in each labeled "group."

We believe that the move away from labeling is part of the inevitable evolution of the field. All areas of education evolve and reform over time. Healey (2005) provided an historical context for changes in special education. He noted that the early 1970s was a time when different groups (parents, educators, legislators) moved with determination to reform special education. These combined efforts resulted in the historic Public Law 94-142, the Education of All Handicapped Children Act, in 1975. Through periodic reauthorizations, the law changed to reflect current theory, practice, and research. Truscott, Catanese, and Abrams (2005) reported concerns and research that lead to current calls for "radical special education reform" (p. 164). It is the nature of the development of a field to experience change. The radical changes in the education of students with special needs that began in the 1970s affected both special and general education, and indirectly, the field of gifted education as well. With the most current reauthorization of the Individuals with Disabilities Education Act in 2004, we are experiencing a change that has the potential to impact education to the same degree that Public Law 94-142 did. This is due to the significant shift in the identification of specific learning disabilities (SLD) within the law:

> Consensus reports and empirical syntheses indicate a need for major changes in the approach to identifying children with SLD. Models that incorporate RtI represent a shift in special education toward goals of better achievement and improved behavioral outcomes for children with SLD. (Office of the Federal Register, 2006, p. 46647)

Principle 1	All children can learn and achieve high standards if given access to a rigorous, standards-based curriculum and research-based instruction.
Principle 2	Intervening at the earliest indication of need is necessary to ensure student success.
Principle 3	A comprehensive system of tiered interventions is essential for addressing the full range of student needs.
Principle 4	Student results improve when ongoing academic and behavioral performance data inform instructional decisions.
Principle 5	Collaboration among educators, families, and community members is the foundation for effective problem solving and instructional decision making.
Principle 6	Ongoing and meaningful family engagement increases successful outcomes for students.

Figure 4.1. Core principles of a Response to Intervention model. Adapted from Colorado Department of Education (2009).

CORE PRINCIPLES OF RTI

Because of the complexity and needs-based nature of RtI, there are a number of different models in practice. Regardless of the model, there is an underlying set of common core principles or beliefs that guide successful practice (see Figure 4.1). These principles, listed below, were adapted from a list developed by the CDE and were based on a review of the literature on RtI as well as practical application of these principles. The intent of this section is to address these principles and discuss how RtI is an excellent way to address the needs of all students, and within that context, the needs of twice-exceptional students.

PRINCIPLE 1: ALL CHILDREN CAN LEARN

Effective instructional strategies are the hallmark of gifted education. Researchers at Mid-continent Research for Education and Learning (McREL) have identified nine instructional strategies through a theory-based meta-analysis. These strategies have a "high probability of enhancing student achievement for all students in all subject areas at all grade levels" (Marzano, Pickering & Pollock, 2001, p. 7). These nine research-based instructional strategies provide some guidance and direction for improving instructional practices in classrooms. The strategies are listed in order of highest to lowest effect:

1. identifying similarities and differences;
2. summarizing and note taking;
3. reinforcing effort and providing recognition;
4. homework and practice;
5. nonlinguistic representations;
6. cooperative learning;
7. setting objectives and providing feedback;
8. generating and testing hypotheses; and
9. questions, cues, and advance organizers (Marzano et al., 2001, p. 7).

These research-based instructional strategies are ones that benefit all students when used consistently in the general classroom. This type of instructional consistency benefits twice-exceptional students in particular because they are more successful in an environment with clear expectations, guidance, and opportunities to problem solve. These instructional strategies, used in conjunction with the Pre-K–Grade 12 Gifted Programming Standards developed and released by the National Association for Gifted Children (NAGC) in 2010, provide a consistent framework to address the needs of gifted students in all educational settings. These standards support an examination of the quality of programming for gifted learners and include both minimum standards and exemplary standards in seven key areas. They serve as a way for districts to set benchmarks as well as to evaluate their programs for gifted learners. A combination of research-based instructional strategies and the Gifted Education Program Standards can contribute to the development of a solid universal tier of instruction for school systems utilizing an RtI framework.

PRINCIPLE 2: EARLY INTERVENTION

A second guiding principle is the idea that intervening at the earliest indication of need is necessary to ensure student success (CDE, 2008). In the case of twice-exceptional students, a significant educational need, whether for acceleration, enrichment, and/or remediation, may not be apparent in the early years of school. Many twice-exceptional students are able to mask their diverse needs until much later in their school experience (McCoach, Kehle, Bray, & Siegle, 2001). It is often the case that their acceleration or enrichment needs may remain undetected until later in their school experience because they have not been put into learning environments that allow for success or that foster interest and motivation for learning. Literature suggests that it is crucial to access the talent and ability of twice-exceptional students as early as possible (Baldwin, 1995; Baum, Cooper, & Neu, 2001; Neu, 2003; Nielsen, 2002; Reis, McGuire, & Neu, 2000; Reis, Neu, & McGuire, 1995; Weinfeld, Barnes-Robinson, Jeweler, & Roffman Shevitz, 2006). A consistent theme has emerged from the literature: "Programmatic interventions suggest the importance of providing these students with a curriculum that accommodates their unique gifts and talents while simultaneously allowing the students to compensate for problematic weaknesses" (Neu, 2003, p. 152). It is fundamental to the success of twice-exceptional students to identify and nurture their gifts and talents (Baum & Owen, 2004).

This principle addresses the need to intervene at the earliest sign of a problem. A problem is defined here as an educational need for acceleration, enrichment, and/or remediation. If caught early enough, remediation for a disability can make a significant difference for a twice-exceptional child and change his school experience to a more positive one. When provided with remediation strategies early, twice-exceptional students can alleviate some of the challenges quickly and may not need long-term intensive support.

PRINCIPLE 3: TIERED INTERVENTIONS

Another crucial principle of an effective RtI model is the inclusion of a comprehensive system of tiered interventions. RtI begins in the universal tier with high-quality instruction and curriculum that all students receive and is intended to address the needs of approximately 80% of the students within that system. Students identified as having an educational need are provided with interventions at increasing levels of duration and intensity. Targeted interventions are used for approximately 10%–15% of students within the system for whom there are needs beyond what is provided at the universal tier. These interventions are provided by a variety of educational personnel including general educators, special educators, gifted educators, and specialists. When there continues to be an educational need, as measured by ongoing progress monitoring with curriculum-based measures (CBM), the intervention is modified or adapted to increase progress or to further enhance the learning of the student. The most intensive tier of intervention is meant to address the needs of about 5%–7% of the students within a system.

The benefits of a multitiered system for twice-exceptional students are significant. The intent of these tiers is to address the varied educational needs of students. Each twice-exceptional student has not only traits and characteristics in the realm of giftedness, but in one or more areas of disability/exceptionality. This combination of strengths and challenges has made it difficult to address the multiple and varied educational needs of students. The RtI/problem-solving process is more fluid than the typical school system of separate programs because all student needs, remedial and advanced, can be addressed. The process allows for a discussion of the whole child, starting with strengths. This multitiered system allows for an ongoing discussion about each student's needs without a push to get the child tested for special education. Interventions can occur without a label.

PRINCIPLE 4: USE OF DATA

Another core principle of RtI that is directly related to the multitiered model is that student results are improved when ongoing academic and behavioral performance data are used to inform instructional decisions (CDE, 2008). The effective use of data in an RtI model is crucial to assist in instructional decisions across the tiers. Screening begins at the universal tier for all students. This practice has great promise for twice-exceptional students. These students "often use their high levels of intelligence to compensate for problematic weaknesses" (Baum & Owen, 2004, p. 160). This compensation acts as a mask over their areas of struggle. With the use of valid, reliable screening instruments, many issues can be detected early and appropriate interventions assigned.

PRINCIPLE 5: COLLABORATION

Another foundational principle of an effective RtI model involves the belief that collaboration among educators, families, and community members is the foundation to effective problem solving and instructional decision making (CDE, 2008). The problem-solving process acts as a way of systematizing the decision-making process to lead to the development of instructional and intervention strategies that will have the highest probability of success. The purpose of having this process in place is to use the data to guide decisions about appropriate interventions and to monitor student progress through those interventions to determine their effectiveness.

To have such a system in place to address the ongoing and changing needs of twice-exceptional students is extremely helpful. Too often, in typical educational systems, interventions are developed but not monitored or modified for effectiveness on a frequent basis. Because of this, weeks—and sometimes months—of instructional opportunities are lost. With the problem-solving process, there are built-in checkpoints to review data and the effectiveness of the interventions, whether they are remedial or advanced learning opportunities.

Collaboration in this process is crucial. This requires a team of professionals and families to work together as partners to identify a measurable outcome for the learner. It is an opportunity to utilize data from a variety of sources to inform the instructional decisions made for a student and to adapt the intervention along the way at appropriate intervals. This type of collaboration has been identified as crucial when addressing the needs of twice-exceptional students. Various studies have pointed to the importance of the balance between remediation and attention to the child's strength (Baldwin, 1995; Baum et al., 2001; Nielsen, 2002; Reis et al., 1995; Weinfeld et al., 2006). Collaboration allows for a shared ownership for student success. General, special, and gifted educators work together to support the needs of students, especially twice-exceptional learners.

PRINCIPLE 6: FAMILY ENGAGEMENT

A final core principle that is a guiding force in an effective RtI model is the belief that ongoing and meaningful family engagement increases the successful outcomes for students. Research supports the principle that families engaged in a positive relationship with schools can have a direct impact on the achievement of students (Henderson & Mapp, 2002). What is true about twice-exceptional students is that they are even more at risk for failure and underachievement without family involvement. Many times families may see a different child at home—much different than the one educators see in a school environment where the child may be feeling less support and success. For this reason, it is the job of parents to advocate for their child and represent their view of his or her strengths and challenges.

The problem-solving format is a perfect venue for such advocacy. In addition, parents must be prepared to provide support at home for academics. Within the RtI/problem-solving process, the parents are at the table and involved in determining the necessary intervention for their child. They will leave the problem-solving meeting with some guidance for home support that is directly related to the chosen intervention. By empowering the family to be part of the solution, the outcomes for the child are more successful.

CASE STUDY

This case study was written utilizing the steps of the RtI problem-solving/consultation model. There are several steps to this problem-solving process that are important for the fidelity and implementation of a successful plan (see Figure 4.2). To help illustrate how this plan might work for any child, but particularly a twice-exceptional student, we will use Brad as a case study.

BACKGROUND INFORMATION

Brad is a likeable, high-energy boy who enjoys conversations with adults. He loves to watch the History Channel on television. His preco-

1. Initial Consultation

Together, the consultant, referring teacher, and/or parent:

- Discuss gathered information from teacher/parent (if a teacher referral, teacher has already been in contact with parent)
- Begin the process of identifying the student's strengths, challenges, and needs
- List abilities and/or problems the student is demonstrating
- Prioritize issues and define the "problem" (remedial and/or advanced) based on data analysis

2. Initial Problem-Solving Team Meeting

Members of the problem-solving team:

- Generate interventions for the problem or ability
- Determine who is going to provide intervention, when it will take place, how often, and in what group
- Determine who will progress monitor and what tool will be used
- Determine, through parent/family input and guidance, what will support or supplement intervention at home
- Schedule the follow-up meeting

3. Intervention Implementation and Progress Monitoring

Consultant, teacher, and parent:

- Continue to communicate regularly about the intervention
- Ensure that the intervention protocol is followed
- Continue to emphasize the shared responsibility for the student's success

4. Follow-Up Consultation

Consultant guides discussion with teacher and interventionist (if different person) to:

- Discuss progress monitoring data, observational data, and report from parent/family
- Adjust aimline when goals are met early
- Prepare for follow-up meeting to ensure a smooth efficient flow

5. Follow-Up Problem-Solving Team Meeting

Members of the problem-solving team:

- Set tone by using data to discuss effectiveness of intervention
- Value teacher and parent input
- Review effectiveness of the intervention plan
- Make decisions about next steps

Figure 4.2. Problem-solving/consultation process. Adapted from the Colorado Department of Education (2009).

cious and highly developed vocabulary, as well as his maturity, caused his preschool teacher and staff to recommend that he skip kindergarten and begin first grade in the fall. His parents were amazed and pleased by this recommendation, and they enrolled him in a private religious school. From the very beginning of first grade, he struggled with academic skills, particularly reading and writing, and was unable to keep up with his classmates. At the end of first grade, it was decided that he was still not ready to move on to second grade and that it would be better for his self-esteem and academic progress if he remained in first grade another year. By the end of September of his second year as a first grader, Brad was so frustrated that he tossed over his chair and desk and ran out of school, determined never to come back. The private school agreed with this sentiment and asked the parents to find a new school. By October Brad was transferred into the local public school. This suburban school had been implementing an RtI/problem-solving approach to meeting the needs of all students for more than 2 years. Brad's new teacher recognized very quickly that he was struggling with reading and writing. He appeared to be very unhappy as demonstrated by negative comments such as "I'm so stupid" or "This work is dumb." He was known to rip up and throw away some of his writing assignments or he would just put his head down on the desk and refuse to complete the assigned task. Because of these behaviors, the classroom teacher set up a meeting with the parents as part of the data-gathering process of RtI to discuss her concerns and to determine their thoughts and ideas about their son's behaviors and progress.

PARENT INFORMATION

The parents reported seeing some very angry behaviors at home when Brad would return from school. These behaviors included his running around in circles and screaming until he would wear himself out and collapse on the floor in tears. In addition, he was also refusing to do any homework even with support from his parents. They agreed with the teacher that a referral requesting an initial consultation would be helpful. Because of the nature of his learning and behavioral issues, the teacher requested an initial consultation and began the referral to the problem-solving team. Due to the concerns about learning and behavior, the special education teacher was assigned to be the consultant.

INITIAL CONSULTATION

The purpose of the initial consultation is to discuss gathered information in order to support the referring teacher and/or parent and to begin the process of identifying the student's strengths, challenges, and needs. The classroom teacher, parent, or school professionals can request assistance. A consultant is assigned to meet with the teacher to discuss the child's specific behaviors, review the academic data, and, if necessary, gather more data to determine the needs of the learner. This may include observing the learner in a variety of settings, evaluating his abilities utilizing a variety of testing and/or screening materials, or gathering more of his classroom work samples. Strengths and needs of the learner will be identified and prioritized by the teacher and the consultant. The problem will be defined and an observable, measurable plan will be developed.

Initial consultation for Brad. The classroom teacher and the consultant met to discuss Brad. The classroom teacher noted that Brad was very animated and participatory during social studies and science. He made many contributions during these classes, often demonstrating knowledge that was very advanced and sophisticated. In fact, he would try to engage her in more in-depth discussions but she could rarely accommodate him because the rest of the class was not at that level. He also liked the conversations and book discussions during literature class/book circle, but he refused to read out loud during any of these classes. In fact, it was very hard to determine his reading issues and level because he refused to take the Dynamic Indicator of Basic Early Literacy Skills (DIBELS) and the reading comprehension screening. In addition, his pencil grip was awkward and his handwriting was large, disjointed, and very difficult to read. He refused to participate in any creative writing activities.

During their meeting, the classroom teacher and the consultant determined that more data was needed. The consultant decided that she would observe him in all of his classes, including social studies and science. She would also attempt to evaluate his reading skills individually in a separate location where he would not have to read in front of other students. They would begin compiling his classwork, including his worksheets in social studies and science to establish a portfolio of his writing. The classroom teacher would ask Brad's mother for any data and work samples that she had from his preschool and first-grade classes. They agreed to collect the data and to meet again in 2 weeks.

At the next meeting, they reviewed the data that they had gathered. The observations were very valuable. The consultant was able to observe Brad's motivation in social studies and science and his attempts to dominate the discussion.

Brad's mother provided valuable information about the lack of reading help that occurred at the private school and the fact that his reading difficulties were seen as a demonstration of willful and inappropriate behavior on his part. Other than his parents reading to him every night before going to bed, his mother noted that he had not been given any special help with his reading.

The consultant completed the reading assessment and was able to identify that Brad had major issues with decoding and that he knew some of the initial consonant sounds but could not identify the vowel sounds. His reading comprehension was very poor because of his attempts to sound out each word but his oral comprehension when the story was read to him was two grade levels above his current placement.

The teacher and the consultant listed all of the existing needs and the accompanying data. When they prioritized the problems and abilities, they determined that they needed to focus on his decoding skills, and they needed to address his interest and passion in social studies and science by involving him in an advanced study activity. The consultant agreed to set up the initial problem-solving team meeting, and the teacher stated that she would call the parents to invite them to participate in the meeting.

INITIAL PROBLEM-SOLVING TEAM MEETING

The purpose of the initial problem-solving team meeting is to generate interventions that are measurable and observable and that address the identified problem or ability. Because the problem identification has occurred at the initial consultation, this meeting can focus on determining the specific interventions; establishing the intensity and duration of the intervention; assigning the person(s) responsible for the interventions; identifying the materials, accommodations, and modifications; and determining the frequency of progress monitoring. Families are considered to be valued members of this team and are often given tasks to accomplish at home that reinforce and support the efforts of the school personnel. At the secondary level, the student is often asked to participate in the meeting. Minutes of the meeting are taken by the assigned note taker and distributed to all participants. If the initial consultation has been effective, the initial problem-solving team meeting should not take more than an hour.

Brad's initial problem-solving team meeting. There were a number of participants in Brad's initial problem-solving team meeting—the classroom teacher, the consultant, the gifted and talented coordinator, the occupational therapist, the reading teacher, the principal, and his parents. Because Brad demonstrated many of the behavioral characteristics of a twice-exceptional student, it was determined that an intervention focusing on his strengths, as well as an intervention to address at least one of his academic challenges, was necessary. After discussing the reasons for Brad's referral and reviewing the data, the problem-solving team determined that the following plans would be put in place (see Figure 4.3 for Brad's continuum of support).

In order to capitalize on Brad's interest in social studies, it was determined that he would develop an independent study. He would be given options to explore a topic of interest related to the social studies curriculum in more depth. Prior to the independent study, he would be given an oral preassessment to ascertain his knowledge of the basic curriculum in this area. He would also be given the opportunity to choose the method of presenting his independent project. He would join a small group of first, second, and third graders who were also working in independent projects with the gifted and talented teacher twice a week for 45 minutes each. In addition, he would be given time to work on his project during social studies class when the other students were working on their assignments. The classroom teacher, with the assistance of the gifted and talented teacher, would design a rubric for grading and monitoring his project. Brad would accompany his class on field trips to the police station, fire station, and the mayor's office during the 4-week social studies

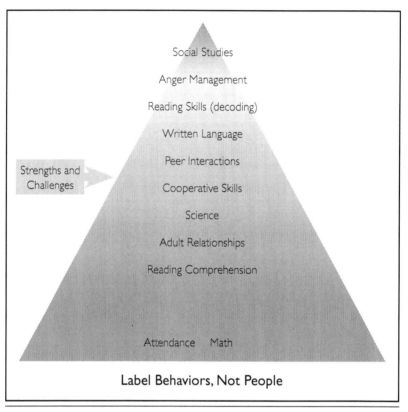

Figure 4.3. RtI continuum of support for Brad. This figure includes Brad's identified academic and behavioral needs for use in the development of an appropriate educational plan.

unit on community. His parents agreed to participate by taking Brad to visit the community library, as well as historical buildings and sites in the area.

The problem-solving committee determined from the data, and from comments that they had heard Brad say, that he was very frustrated with his inability to read quickly and well. Although the classroom teacher was already teaching phonics as part of the reading/literacy block every day, it was decided that Brad would benefit more from a different targeted intervention designed to teach decoding skills in a sequential and multisensory manner. The reading teacher was already working with two other students on this intervention during that block, and she felt that he would fit nicely with the other students. Brad participated in this group 5 days a week for 30 minutes per day. The reading teacher also worked with the classroom teacher to alert her to what phonetic skills were being addressed weekly so that she could reinforce them during classroom activities.

In addition to the two plans that focused on Brad's strengths and concerns, the committee decided that it needed more information about his difficulties with writing and behavior. The parents granted permission to allow the occupational therapist to do an assessment and the school psychologist to conduct a functional behavioral analysis (FBA).

It was agreed that the problem-solving committee would meet in 3 weeks to determine if progress was being made.

INTERVENTION AND PROGRESS MONITORING

Once the problem-solving meeting takes place, it is time to begin the intervention and progress-monitoring phase. It is important during this phase for the plan that is developed during the meeting to be implemented with fidelity. The consultant will continue to be involved as a support to the classroom teacher.

Brad's intervention and progress monitoring. The classroom teacher and the reading teacher met that afternoon to discuss the reading curriculum and decided that Brad would start with the new phonics group on Monday. The teacher was given the lesson plans for the week so that she could support both Brad and the other two students during the week in class. The two teachers agreed to meet every Friday to review the curriculum and progress monitoring data.

The day after the problem-solving meeting, the classroom teacher gave Brad his social studies oral pretest. It was determined that he indeed knew the information needed to pass the assessment at the end of the Pilgrim unit. The day after the classroom teacher alerted his parents, she and the gifted and talented teacher met with Brad to discuss the plan. Brad was delighted that he was going to be able to work on a special project. Because the current topic of the social studies curriculum was community services, Brad chose to compare and contrast the community services provided during the colonial period versus those in his current New England town. He was given options of how he could present his independent study. Brad chose to create a slideshow presentation, and he already had some ideas that he wanted to incorporate into the presentation.

FOLLOW-UP CONSULTATION

The follow-up consultation is important in order to determine whether all of the plans are being implemented and to determine if adjustments need to be made. The assigned consultant can meet with the parents, classroom teacher, and/or the teachers who are providing intervention services. The consultant will also look at the data being collected because they will be the input necessary for making any adjustments during the next problem-solving meeting.

Brad's follow-up consultation. The special education teacher had been assigned as the consultant for Brad's case. Two weeks into the intervention, she arranged a meeting with the classroom teacher, the reading teacher, and the gifted and talented teacher to determine Brad's progress with the new plans. The classroom teacher reported that Brad was responding well to the social studies plan. He looked forward to going to the gifted and talented resource room twice a week and he proudly showed her the progress he was making on his slideshow presentation. The gifted and talented teacher concurred that he was taking responsibility for his project and was following the outline that they had developed. Both teachers felt that he would have his project completed by the 3-week deadline. They also noted that Brad's parents had been very helpful with getting him resource books and books on CD at the local library.

The reading teacher stated that Brad was actively participating in the reading program and that it appeared from his progress that he was responding positively to the sequential and multisensory approach to phonics. He had at this point learned several consonant sounds but was still having difficulty with the short vowel sounds. The classroom teacher noted that even though he was making progress, he was very unhappy in her reading group. Because he comprehended far better than he was able to read as noted in the testing prior to the initial problem-solving meeting, she wanted to explore ways to allow him to be in a more sophisticated reading group because of his need to discuss and analyze the reading passages.

The consultant asked about Brad's parents and whether they had noted any changes. The classroom teacher indicated that she had been talking to Brad's mother every Friday informally via e-mail. She reported that his behavior was still very unpredictable at home: Sometimes he would become upset and irritable, which led to crying and tantrums, and other times he was sweet, agreeable, and willing to work on his special social studies project. He was still refusing to do any other type of work.

FOLLOW-UP PROBLEM-SOLVING TEAM MEETING

At this meeting, there should be enough data to determine whether progress is being made, to review the student's response to intervention and to discuss next steps. The teacher, consultant, and parents have an opportunity to review the data together and to make decisions about continuing the current plan or to change plans based on information collected.

Brad's follow-up problem-solving team meeting. The follow-up problem-solving team consisted of the same members that met during the initial problem-solving team meeting.

The team started by discussing Brad's social studies independent project in which he was going to develop a slideshow presentation. It was determined that this had been a very successful plan based on the results of his final project as he had produced 10 relevant slides. He worked very effectively with the gifted and talented teacher, was able to follow the outline and to work independently in the classroom during social studies, and was able to demonstrate an increased understanding and knowledge about the subject. Because data demonstrated success, it was decided that another project with the gifted and talented teacher was appropriate.

The reading teacher reviewed the data from Brad's daily work in the phonics group. In 3 weeks, he had learned four initial consonant sounds and was practicing four more. Although he was able to identify the initial consonant sounds, he was still having difficulty with consonant-vowel-consonant (c-v-c) words because of the short vowel sounds.

It was decided that the reading teacher and the classroom teacher would continue to work on the specific skills related to c-v-c and short vowel sounds. They also discussed that he may need a reading program with a different approach in the future in order to acquire the vowel sounds if the data demonstrated that need, but they felt that it was too soon to make that decision because they still did not have enough data. They decided to monitor his progress closely.

The classroom and reading teachers also noted that even though Brad was struggling with decoding, his reading assessment information indicated that he was able to comprehend at least two grade levels above his actual grade placement. Brad was complaining during reading group that the stories were boring and was either dominating the group, making fun of the stories, or refusing to participate. Because this issue had been discussed during consultation, the special education teacher had done some checking prior to the meeting. She had talked to the high school principal about utilizing an honors student who needed to earn community service credit. The student would record Brad's reading assignments and questions into a tape recorder so that Brad could listen to them and be prepared to participate in the highest level reading group on a daily basis for 30 minutes. Because the end of the first semester was in 3 weeks, they decided that it would be helpful to meet at that time.

The RtI process will continue during the year as the problem-solving team and Brad's assigned consultant assess the data, review his progress, and determine whether intervention is still needed or should be modified. The important element for a twice-exceptional student is that both his strengths and his challenges are addressed. During that process, Brad may receive interventions that are at any one of the tiers but the decisions will be based on his needs and the data gathered through the interventions. Ultimately, if these interventions are not sufficient to meet Brad's needs as currently established, and he demonstrates the need for ongoing intensive support to be successful, then he may be identified as a student with a disability and an Individualized Education Program (IEP) would be developed through this same process. He may also be identified as a student who needs gifted and talented ongoing services.

CONCLUSION

Brad's case study illustrates why RtI is a promising fit for the child who has gifts as well as learning and emotional issues. Instead of thinking about putting a label on Brad and sending him to special education, the classroom teacher focused on his needs first. She was aware that she needed to identify the problem and, with the help of the consultant and the problem-solving team, find a way to assist him with the evidence-based curriculum and activities that were available to her and the team. The core principles of RtI are the driving force behind this process and evident throughout. With a twice-exceptional child like Brad, the goal is always to focus on both the gift and the academic or behavioral need.

The research identified in this chapter has stated that it is important that educators and parents find ways to emphasize each student's strengths. These students, like all students, need to have high-level instruction and academic challenges. At the same time, twice-exceptional students must receive appropriate remediation and help for the areas that interfere with their progress. As a result of the problem-solving/consultation process, Brad was able to receive early intervention in reading and still participate in higher level thinking activities such as the social studies independent project.

The problem-solving team was still in the process of evaluating the data to determine whether he needed modifications or intensive support in writing. Because the RtI process is ongoing and focuses on student needs, the problem-solving team would continue to review Brad's progress, and the interventionist, along with the consultant, would adjust the intensity and type of services and materials along the way. They might determine that Brad needs more support within the most intensive tier of interventions for his reading and writing but that he is able to function with his classmates in an activity at the universal tier in science and math. These decisions will be based on his needs, not his label. Because interventions are based on the needs of students within individual systems, determination of the level of the intervention will be dependent on the system.

At some point in the process, there may be a time when a disability is suspected and it may be evident that Brad needs ongoing targeted and/or intensive support to be successful. At this point, a recommendation for consideration for a full and individual evaluation would be made.

Because Response to Intervention is a multifaceted approach, it addresses the comprehensive academic and behavioral needs of all students. Inherent in its design is the focus on both student strengths and challenges in a variety of ways. Because of the complex needs of twice-exceptional students, the RtI/problem-solving process is a very promising system that will meet their needs for high-level instruction and appropriate remediation. The old system of "wait to fail" identification and service delivery is not an adequate model for any student, and it is particularly ineffective with twice-exceptional students because of their unique needs.

As demonstrated by the research, there is an urgency to intervene early with twice-exceptional students and to focus on their strengths. The core principles of a Response to Intervention model allow the needs of twice-exceptional students to be directly addressed. These principles direct the focus of an entire system to success for all students. As the principles indicate, this includes an intentional emphasis on early intervention through a multitiered approach based on student needs. This requires a move away from the silos of education into a more collaborative effort and a need to create an "every-ed" approach. With an increased emphasis on student outcomes and data-driven instructional decisions in an RtI model, this will lead to a much more successful school experience for twice-exceptional students.

REFERENCES

Baldwin, L. (1995). *Portraits of gifted learning disabled students: A longitudinal study* (Unpublished doctoral dissertation). Teachers College, Columbia University, New York, NY.

Baum, S., Cooper, C., & Neu, T. (2001). Dual differentiation: An approach for meeting the curricular needs of gifted students with learning disabilities. *Psychology in the Schools, 38,* 477–490.

Baum, S. M., & Owen, S. V. (2004). *To be gifted & learning disabled.* Mansfield Center, CT: Creative Learning Press.

Cole, R. W. (2008). *Educating everybody's children: Diverse teaching strategies for diverse learners.* Alexandria, VA: Association for Supervision and Curriculum Development.

Colorado Department of Education. (2008). *Response to Intervention: A practitioner's guide to implementation.* Denver, CO: Author.

Colorado Department of Education. (2009). *Response to Intervention: Problem-solving/consultation process training video guide.* Denver, CO: Author.

Council for Exceptional Children. (2008). *Council for Exceptional Children 2008 policy manual.* Arlington, VA: Author.

Education for All Handicapped Children Act of 1975, Pub. Law 94-142 (November 29, 1975).

Healey, W. C. (2005). The learning disability phenomenon in pursuit of axioms. *Learning Disability Quarterly, 28,* 115–118.

Henderson, A. T., & Mapp, K. L. (2002). *A new wave of evidence: The impact of school, family and community connections on student achievement.* Austin, TX: Southwest Educational Development Lab.

Individuals with Disabilities Education Improvement Act, Pub. Law 108-446 (December 3, 2004).

Lauchlan, F., & Boyle, C., (2007). Is the use of labels in special education helpful? *Support for Learning, 22*(1), 36–42.

Marzano, R. J., Pickering, D. J., & Pollock, J. E. (2001). *Classroom instruction that works: Research-based strategies for increasing student achievement.* Alexandria, VA: Association for Supervision and Curriculum Development.

McCoach, D. B., Kehle, T. J., Bray, M. A., & Siegle, D. (2001). Best practices in the identification of gifted students with learning disabilities. *Psychology in the Schools, 38,* 403–411.

National Association for Gifted Children. (2010). *2010 pre-K–grade 12 gifted programming standards* Retrieved from http://www.nagc.org/uploadedFiles/Information_and_Resources/Gifted_Program_Standards/K-12%20programming%20standards.pdf

National Association of State Directors of Special Education. (2005). *Response to Intervention: Policy considerations and implementation.* Alexandria, VA: Author.

Neu, T. (2003). When the gifts are camouflaged by disability: Identifying and developing the talent in gifted students with disabilities. In J. A. Castellano (Ed.), *Special populations in gifted education: Working with diverse gifted learners* (pp. 151–162). Boston, MA: Allyn & Bacon.

Nielsen, M. E. (2002). Gifted students with learning disabilities: Recommendations for identification and programming. *Exceptionality, 10*(2), 93–111.

Office of the Federal Register. (2006). Specific learning disabilities. *Rules and Regulations 71*(156), 46647.

Reis, S. M., McGuire, J. M., & Neu, T. W. (2000). Compensation strategies used by high ability students with learning disabilities who succeed in college. *Gifted Child Quarterly, 44,* 123–134.

Reis, S. M., Neu, T. W., & McGuire, J. M. (1995). *Talents in two places: Case studies of high ability students with learning disabilities who have achieved.* Storrs: University of Connecticut, The National Research Center on the Gifted and Talented.

Renzulli, J. S., Reis, S. M., & Smith, L. H. (1981). *The revolving door identification model.* Mansfield Center, CT: Creative Learning Press.

Truscott, S. D., Catanese, A. M., & Abrams, L. M. (2005). The evolving context of special education classification in the United States. *School Psychology International, 26,* 162–177.

Weinfeld, R., Barnes-Robinson, L., Jeweler, S., & Roffman Shevitz, B. (2006). *Smart kids with learning difficulties: Overcoming obstacles and realizing potential.* Waco, TX: Prufrock Press.

CHAPTER 5

RtI for Gifted Students: Policy Implications

Elissa F. Brown and Sherry H. Abernethy

Response to Intervention (RtI) has become an instructional practice employed predominantly in general education classrooms across the United States as a direct result of the reauthorization of the Individuals with Disabilities Education Act (IDEA, 2004). RtI has implications for gifted education as a framework for policy development because it is an integrative approach to classroom practices that modify high-quality instruction based upon students' academic or behavioral needs (National Association of State Directors of Special Education [NASDSE], 2007). It is based on a public health model of intervention in which tiers of increasingly intense interventions are directed at correspondingly smaller and smaller population segments (Mellard & Johnson, 2008). Students are systemically and frequently monitored, data are evaluated, and goals and evidence-based interventions are implemented in order to preclude a student from being identified and ultimately placed in special education services. The focus on the three aspects of (a) screening and prevention, (b) early intervention, and (c) disability determination underscores it as an important construct because of its potential to help schools provide appropriate learning experiences for all students. At a practical level, RtI is just sound, effective teaching. It is preassessing students through a strategic process, making modifications in accordance to students' displayed needs, and monitoring student progress employing a tiered approach in order for higher student outcomes to be realized. One might ask, "Don't teachers of the gifted do this already?"

There are many program and curricular models in gifted education: Some address a tiered approach to instruction and interventions, while other models address curricular or grouping strategies (VanTassel-Baska & Brown, 2009). Regardless of the program or curricular model employed in gifted education classrooms, it is typically not implemented consistently across the country or even within the same school district. As a field, gifted education does not endorse any one approach to serving students because of the range of student abilities and resulting concomitant diverse needs; therefore, service delivery in gifted education is still heavily teacher dependent. Yet, many of the components of RtI are employed in gifted education, albeit inconsistently, such as preassessment. The use of preassessment in gifted education diagnostically to evaluate a gifted learner's performance prior to instruction has been widely used in classrooms to determine an authentic level of achievement and then implement pedagogical modifications matched to individual students. Preassessment has been documented as an effective tool with gifted students (Callahan, 2005), especially if educators accept the premise that gifted students have already mastered approximately 30% of the curriculum to be taught (U.S. Department of Education, 1993). Although some of the current gifted curricular and instructional models embed key components of RtI within them, they are not implemented in a coherent or strategic fashion and educational policies undergirding both RtI and effective practices in gifted education are scant. Unless RtI has leadership and support from district and/or state policies, it will not be implemented with fidelity and will lose its potential as a framework for overall student achievement. Leadership and policies become the infrastructure for RtI to not only become operational but also systemic. Therefore, a need exists to create state and local policies that allow for the congruence of RtI and gifted education.

RATIONALE FOR POLICY INITIATIVES

The stance that policies delineating the use of RtI for gifted students are needed is based on three major assumptions about the role of policies for the gifted. First, policies for gifted learners have been relegated to state and local initiatives, typically linked to funding priorities. Without a district or state policy, implementation of RtI remains idiosyncratic, lacks fidelity, and rests on the backs of a passionate few who value its inherent potential for student achievement. Employing RtI as a vehicle for gifted education service and delivery would require a policy that speaks to the flexibility of curricular, instructional, and assessment practices.

The second assumption is that gifted education needs coherency among program components such as identification and services linked to professional development and teacher preparation. Frequently, due to a lack of adequate resources, gifted education has been a fragmented enterprise at the local level, perhaps a pull-out program in language arts at the elementary school, an ability-grouped mathematics class at the middle school, or a few designated Advanced Placement (AP) courses at the high school, each operating independently from the other and each not necessarily linked to the identification processes employed to find gifted students and develop their potential. In order to achieve a coherent framework for gifted programming that includes RtI as an approach, the field must employ a systematic framework for improvement and must develop policies that support implementation and program improvement in a coherent fashion.

The third assumption is that the development of policy that speaks to RtI's implication for gifted students links gifted education to the broader reform efforts occurring within special and general education. Gifted education can ill afford to be an "island unto oneself." Clune (1993) noted that to sustain an educational reform agenda, policy development is an essential component. Gifted education historically has used the special education model as a basis for programming and identification, and has used the psychological measurement orientation as a means of encompassing student outliers. At the same time, gifted education has attempted to incorporate general educational principles of curriculum design, teacher expertise, and organizational support structures. If gifted education is to continue and advance as a field, it will have to embrace the world of general education, its models, and its curriculum reform while not abandoning the exceptionality concept that defines the nature of the population (VanTassel-Baska, 2003). Therefore, a policy that can create a hybrid combining the best practices of special, general, and gifted education can ensure sound practices built on a research base.

POTENTIAL RTI COMPONENTS FOR GIFTED POLICY DEVELOPMENT

At this point, policy development and implementation of coherency among policy components in gifted education has been limited. However, by linking gifted policies to RtI and other special or general education practices, the field can reach consensus on policy components that could serve as a template for program and student improvement. Table 5.1 explores the components for policy interface that speak to the core components and stages in RtI, implications for gifted education, and areas for policy development.

SCREENING/PREVENTION

Universal screening as the first key component of RtI is a corollary for screening and nurturing potential in gifted students. One major difference, however, is that traditionally RtI screening has been a way to assess for deficits, due to its original authorization through IDEA (2004). In gifted education, screening usually precedes a more formal approach to identification, is ongoing and comprehensive, and allows schools and teachers a more informal opportunity to assess students' skills and abilities within the classroom context. One of the considerations though, with screening for giftedness, is to use measures that allow for multiple levels of growth to be displayed. If using a standardized measure for universal screening, then a ceiling effect with this population is an issue and should

TABLE 5.1
COMPONENTS OF RTI AND THE IMPLICATIONS FOR GIFTED EDUCATION AND POLICY DEVELOPMENT

Components of RtI	Implications for Gifted	Areas for Policy Development
Screening/ prevention (Universal screening: assessing the core)	• Baseline screening is conducted for all students to determine talent pool and potentiality • Preassessment is used to determine prerequisite knowledge and skills • Formative and curriculum-based assessment approaches are routinely employed • Enrichment and academic activities building upon students' areas of strengths are implemented in response to universal screening of student strengths	• Early identification policies that call for nurturing potential • Policy for ensuring rigor, enrichment, and customization is provided for all students • Early identification policies for ensuring that historically underserved populations (culturally and linguistically diverse, economically disadvantaged, and twice-exceptional) are proactively sought
Early intervention	• Discerning individual precocity and making modifications accordingly, with individuals or small groups of students	
Disability/ability determination	• Identifying based on ability determination	• Policy on off-grade-level testing for highly gifted
Tiered service delivery	• Providing services that match learner abilities and interests • Ensuring that the intensity of services (tiered instruction) match the learning rate and depth of the gifted learner	• Policy that matches service delivery to identification or area(s) of ability • Advanced content and other resources are available for teachers
Fidelity of implementation	• Ensuring coherency among program components such as identification and service, personnel preparation, and program evaluation, as well as ensuring that what gets implemented is research based	• Evaluation/accountability policy for monitoring program delivery and fidelity of services

TABLE 5.1, CONTINUED

Professional development	• Providing professional development for different stakeholders as well as encouraging or requiring teachers of the gifted to have a gifted license or add-on endorsement • Professional development for administrators on classroom expectations, parent involvement, and overall school reform	• Policy for teacher development, licensure, and professional development of all personnel involved with gifted students • Policy/standards developed for school and district leaders
Parent involvement	• Communicating and involving parents in gifted programs or as part of a local steering committee • Parents may be part of a local committee to develop or revise local plans for the gifted	• Policy on involving parents either as part of a local steering committee; to develop and revise local plans; or other mechanism ensuring parent involvement and communication

be taken into consideration. When choosing measures to access the core, teachers should choose materials that allow for above-grade-level growth to be observed or displayed. RtI screening is based on the core curriculum as the source of data and frequently, the core curriculum in most schools and states is pitched at grade-level competencies. Therefore, employing above-grade-level core curriculum for universal screening with gifted students is necessary. Ensuring the academic engagement of students at a high level would speak to providing challenging instructional approaches and content. Gifted education could readily adopt some of the screening practices employed in RtI as screening practices for nurturing potential by considering students' authentic responses to curriculum prior to formal identification. Most states do not have a formal policy for screening in gifted education but it is implied within their identification policy. Early identification policies that call for nurturing potential in historically underserved populations (i.e., culturally and linguistically diverse, economically disadvantaged, and twice-exceptional students) would shore up and formalize a process in which all students are universally screened. Schools could implement universal screening as a precursor for identification or as an instructional strategy for ongoing formative assessment to adjust curricular approaches in response to student needs and learning precocities. Employing universal screening as best practice allows teachers to modify curricular and instructional approaches in response to student readiness.

EARLY INTERVENTION

Attention to identification issues receives the greatest emphasis in all state regulations in gifted education. States are employing more equitable approaches and procedures for identification, seeking to incorporate language that honors a diverse student population (Brown, Avery, VanTassel-Baska, Worley, & Stambaugh, 2006). Universal screening that includes early intervention could be incorporated into an identification policy that calls for casting a wide net and using early intervention strategies in considering talent propensities of early learners and seeking potential in traditionally underrepresented populations. Early intervention provides a proactive stance for teachers because as soon as a gifted student demonstrates mastery in a particular skill area or domain, a teacher can readily adjust instruction upward.

TIERED SERVICE DELIVERY

Another component of RtI that interfaces with gifted education once a student has been identified for gifted services is the degree to which services are linked to learners' skills, interests, and learning profiles. A policy on service delivery being directly linked to learners and their resulting educational needs strengthens gifted education because it begins to provide coherency among programming aspects, such as identification and service. In gifted education, state policies on appropriate programs and services are less prominent, and frequently, if they exist, are not connected to identification. In the RtI model currently in place in many states, service delivery is tiered and based on the intensity of need. For example, if a student requires intensive reading remediation based on earlier screening measures, it is provided. Often in the field of gifted education, a school system may have a service delivery model such as a pull-out resource room that focuses on enrichment activities that may or may not have anything to do with the learner. Rather, scheduling or teacher preferences dictate how students are served. Services for gifted learners must be linked to each student's level of achievement in a domain area to ensure student growth. Tiered services in gifted education should be linked to student strengths, not deficits. However, due to the variance of giftedness, a tiered model could combine elements of both. Policy development linking service delivery around the notion of student customization would provide the necessary support for a teacher to differentiate based on student needs.

FIDELITY OF IMPLEMENTATION

A fourth area in which RtI has implications for gifted education is the area of fidelity of implementing services and overall fidelity of program components. Progress monitoring, as a key component in RtI, is a scientifically based practice of assessing students' performance on a regular basis. Progress monitoring helps school teams make ongoing decisions about instruction. In an era of accountability, implementing an array of services with fidelity cannot be understated. Providing evidence-based instruction resulting in student learning has been found to be almost nonexistent in gifted evaluation studies. VanTassel-Baska and Feng (2004) found that there was an absence of data on student learning, particularly from a systemic perspective, across seven gifted program evaluations conducted statewide and in local school districts. Data-based decision making has become a familiar term in education, yet monitoring the degree to which instructional and curricular approaches are implemented is still an area that needs further development. Two fundamental types of fidelity need to be monitored: student and program. The former deals with ensuring that the tiered services and intensity and pace of instruction are linked to students' strengths and needs. The latter relates to all of the program components being coherent, comprehensive, and driving program improvement. Student and program evaluations must be coupled with professional development, leadership support, and a communication plan.

PROFESSIONAL DEVELOPMENT

Teacher and leadership preparation is another key component necessary to ensure program improvement and a standard of quality instruction in gifted education. Access to trained teachers is especially critical because research has documented that general classroom teachers make very few, if any, modifications for academically talented learners (Westberg, Archambault, Dobyns, & Salvin, 1993). Teachers who do receive specialized training are more likely to provide differentiated curricular and instructional approaches that meet the needs of gifted learners. Leadership training for school and district leaders should be strategically linked to the school's and district's improvement planning process. If policies exist on teacher or administrator preparation, they often lack specificity in respect to content standards or involvement with a state's higher educational community. Moreover, policies typically do not link staff development with teacher performance nor delineate the issue of differentiation of content standards. In 2006, the National Council for Accreditation of Teacher Education (NCATE) adopted standards collaboratively developed by the National Association for Gifted Children (NAGC) and the Council for Exceptional Children (CEC). These national standards for university programs that prepare teachers of the gifted represent a consensus on what teachers should know and be able to do.

PARENT INVOLVEMENT

Last, parent involvement is a key component that interfaces with RtI. In the Response to Intervention model, one of the benefits for parents is that they see how their child is doing, compared to peers, and how the child's class measures up to other classes in the same grade. They can get these results on a regular basis from their school. If class scores are decreasing, for instance, questions will be raised about the quality of teaching in that class; thus, classroom teachers are more accountable for their instruction. Gifted education could adopt this approach to help ensure that fidelity of implementation with parent support occurs. In gifted education, typical parent involvement is either as a member of a local parent task force or steering committee or as a participant at an annual meeting that outlines the gifted program. In the RtI model, parents are involved throughout the process, thereby becoming partners in the enterprise.

IMPLEMENTATION OF RTI IN NORTH CAROLINA

North Carolina, like many other states, has recognized this integrative approach to structured levels of support and solid instruction. Although RtI originated from the reauthorization of IDEA (2004) as a process for identifying specific learning disabilities (SLD), North Carolina has chosen to focus implementation of this initiative as a vehicle to increase academic and behavioral achievement for all learners through working with regular education and classroom teachers. At present, this model is not being employed in gifted education, but a state education agency steering committee convened in May 2010 with the purpose of conceptualizing how RtI can be a framework implemented across the educational spectrum, including gifted education.

Presently, RtI is being implemented in general education classrooms, predominantly at the elementary level, across 120 school systems, including charter schools. The practice of RtI as a four-tier model of problem solving in North Carolina began in 2004, with pilots in five school systems. The pilots were chosen through an application process. These school systems represented a geographic cross-section of North Carolina, which included varied size, location, and student performance levels. The focus on RtI for these pilot sites began with intensive training in problem solving, curriculum-based assessment, awareness of scientific research-based interventions in curriculum areas, positive behavior support, planning, and facilitation. After the initial training and beginning stages of implementation by the pilots, training was then expanded to other school systems in the state, through an additional application process. To date, 320 schools in 120 school systems have participated in state-level training. Currently, 24 school systems across North Carolina with a total count of 62 elementary schools are fully implementing RtI for SLD eligibility. Several secondary schools are moving toward full implementation within the next school year. Preliminary data are currently being collected from the 62 schools fully implementing RtI. Data are being collected on the following RtI components: highest tier of intervention, performance on end-of-year state assessments in reading and math, student retention and eligibility for exceptional children services, and parent involvement.

Although originally introduced as an alternative to eligibility determination of SLD, schools are finding that this model enables them to look at the performance of all students. Although the training and implementation in North Carolina to date has been to preclude students from being identified with SLD and to avoid exceptional children categorization, discussions have ensued around the applicability to all learners, even those performing above grade level or who have the potential to perform above grade level. When schools assess their core instruction, they identify not only students who are lacking in foundational skills but also students who are in need of enrichment and expanded instruction beyond their current grade-level curriculum. The potential for embedding the RtI model exists for supporting all students, even gifted learners, through a structured model of multilevel support. Two essential ingredients in a multilevel support system are policy development and leadership training.

ACTION STEPS FOR POLICY DEVELOPMENT

In order to begin considering how RtI and gifted education can inform each other to ensure that gifted students' needs are met within the RtI framework, a review of current policies—in addition to developing new policies—is needed. The following action steps for policy development provide guiding questions to frame local or state actions when determining the best course of policy options being considered.

1. *Convene a task force.* Organize (local or state) a representative sample of stakeholders to examine current policies and identify potential areas (e.g., curriculum) for policy development. Stakeholder representation should include gifted educators, special educators, and general educators.

2. *Review current policies.* What policies currently exist at state or local levels? Are the current policies comprehensive or inclusive of gifted students, even those from traditionally underrepresented populations? Do the policies link or align to the broader local or state context? Do gifted education policies connect to general education or special education policies in appropriate and meaningful ways?

3. *Assess the implications of creating a new or revising policy.* How are different stakeholders related to the new policy? Would there be any unintended consequences as a result of the revised or new policy? What assumptions does the new or revised policy communicate?

4. *Create or revise policies.* Create a policy that speaks to screening for potential and includes all growth (below grade level, at grade level, and above grade level) as well as providing tiered services that respond to individual needs. Is the policy inclusive of all learners? Does the policy consider grouping, curricular, and instructional modifications? Does the policy allow for horizontal and vertical articulation? Does it convey the school's or district's vision for student success? Is the new/revised policy either adding value to existing policies or filling a policy vacuum?

5. *Take into account implementation considerations.* What are the implications for budget? What mechanisms are in place for communicating, disseminating, and providing technical assistance to ensure the operationalization of the new/revised policy?

6. *Study the fidelity of policy implementation.* Determine policy efficacy through gathering student and program data.

RtI serves as a valuable framework for conversations about policy development because of its potential utility in providing appropriate learning experiences for all students matched to their areas of strength, as well as early identification of students who lack an appropriate match of instructional and curricular choices. Developing a set of action steps for policy development is a way to undergird school practices with the necessary infrastructure. To ensure that policies are written and procedures are put into place, leadership training and support is paramount.

LEADERSHIP TRAINING

An unintended consequence of policy development is that educational practices outpace policies; therefore, leadership support for RtI at school, district, and state levels must occur. When applying RtI through a gifted lens, school leaders should receive training focused on the components of classroom implementation and expectations for student performance. For example, they should be able to observe teachers utilizing screening, formative assessment, and effective instructional practices that build upon students' precocities and areas of strengths. They should observe data-based decision making and academic engaged time (AET), and see a variety of techniques being employed in the classroom. School leaders should have an understanding of how RtI can improve the academic performance of all students in the school and be able to communicate that to parents. School leaders should understand that gifted students require differentiated instruction and curricular approaches that may intensify as students progress through the material. Lastly, school leaders should recognize that moving beyond grade-level standards at a pace and depth commensurate with the student's needs is not only acceptable, but also necessary if RtI is to work in gifted education. At the district level, leaders should shape policies and guidelines that support school implementation. In gifted education, the role of administrators can make or break a program. Because of the tenuous nature of funding, teacher preparation, and political priorities, the role of gifted program administrators cannot be understated. District leaders, therefore, would need to be advocates for RtI and its application to gifted education.

CONCLUSION

RtI is the practice of (a) providing high-quality instruction/intervention matched to student needs and (b) using learning rate over time and level of performance to (c) make important educational decisions (Batsche, Kavale, & Kovaleski, 2006). In the absence of federal laws or mandates governing gifted education, state and local policy, coupled with effective leadership, are the cornerstones driving gifted education programming in school systems across the United States. This need for coherence, which address the components of RtI, is an opportunity to bring together a comprehensive perspective using the lens of special education, gifted education, and general education in creating policies that address differentiation, tiered services, and teacher education. As the use of state standards and accountability measures intensify, the field of gifted education will find it necessary to use policies as the base for creating an infrastructure to support student growth. The way educators approach the practice of education is experiencing tidal waves. There are competing demands for limited resources. Educators can ill afford to operate on separate agendas if they want to address the need for developing optimal opportunities for our best learners. The essential question is how to embrace the betterment of all learners, including the gifted. As a result, considering a model such as RtI affords the field an opportunity to partner with regular and special education in developing policies undergirded by research that are more dynamic and comprehensive in nature by merging and integrating the best of each field. Gifted learners'—and indeed all learners'—educational futures depend upon it.

REFERENCES

Batsche, G., Kavale, K., & Kovaleski, J. (2006). Competing views: A dialogue on response to intervention. *Assessment for Effective Intervention, 32,* 6–19.

Brown, E., Avery, L., VanTassel-Baska, J., Worley, B., & Stambaugh, T. (2006). A five-state analysis of gifted education policy. *Roeper Review, 29,* 11–23.

Callahan, C. M. (2005). Making the grade or achieving the goal? In F. A. Karnes & S. M. Bean (Eds.), *Methods and materials for teaching the gifted* (2nd ed., pp. 211–244). Waco, TX: Prufrock Press.

Clune, W. H. (1993). The best path to systemic educational policy: Standard/centralized or differentiated/decentralized. *Educational Evaluation and Policy Analysis, 15,* 233–254.

Individuals with Disabilities Education Improvement Act, Pub. Law 108-446 (December 3, 2004).

Mellard, D. F., & Johnson, E. (2008). *RTI: A practitioner's guide to implementing Response to Intervention.* Thousand Oaks, CA: Corwin Press.

National Association for Gifted Children/Council for Exceptional Children. (2006). *NAGC-CEC teacher knowledge and skill standards for gifted and talented education.* Retrieved from http://www.ncate.org/public/programStandards.asp?ch=4

National Association of State Directors of Special Education. (2007). *Response to Intervention: Research for practice.* Alexandria, VA: Author.

U.S. Department of Education. (1993). *National excellence: A case for developing America's talent.* Washington, DC: U.S. Government Printing Office.

VanTassel-Baska, J. (2003). *Curriculum planning and instructional design for gifted learners.* Denver, CO: Love.

VanTassel-Baska, J., & Brown, E. (2009). An analysis of gifted education curricular models. In F. A. Karnes & S. M. Bean (Eds.), *Methods and materials for teaching the gifted* (3rd ed., pp. 79–105). Waco, TX: Prufrock Press.

VanTassel-Baska, J., & Feng, A. (2004). *Designing and utilizing evaluation for gifted program improvement.* Waco, TX: Prufrock Press.

Westberg, K. L., Archambault, F. X., Dobyns, S. M., & Salvin, T. J.

(1993). The classroom practices observational study. *Journal for the Education of the Gifted, 16,* 120–146.

CHAPTER 6

Assessing Your School's RtI Model in Serving Gifted Students

Susan K. Johnsen

Response-to-intervention (RtI) is the practice of providing high-quality instruction to *all* students based on their needs. Are gifted and talented students included in your school's RtI model? Do they receive intensive services? Is their progress monitored? Are teachers in gifted education included in the decision-making process? This chapter will address these questions and others to help educators assess important components of their school's RtI model in determining if it provides for gifted and talented students. Components to be assessed include (a) the overall model, (b) how student progress is monitored, (c) tiers of service, (d) curriculum and instructional practices, and (e) collaboration (see Figure 6.1).

OVERALL MODEL

_____ Is your school's standard protocol model flexible?

_____ Does your school use an RtI model that focuses on problem solving?

MONITORING STUDENT PROGRESS

_____ Does your school collect data on the students' strengths as well as their weaknesses?

_____ Do assessments have an adequate ceiling so that advanced students' growth can be measured?

_____ Is information collected frequently?

TIERED LEVELS OF SERVICE

_____ Are services at each level based on student need rather than student label?

_____ Is the Tier 1 curriculum rigorous enough for gifted and academically advanced students to show their strengths?

_____ Are above-grade-level materials and assessments available to academically advanced or gifted students at each tier of service?

_____ Are students able to receive both special education and gifted education services?

_____ Do comprehensive assessments that are used for identification address both strengths and weaknesses?

CURRICULUM AND INSTRUCTIONAL PRACTICES

_____ Does differentiation occur at each tier?

_____ Does the school allow acceleration into above-grade-level content?

_____ Does the curriculum provide challenge for each student?

_____ Are there opportunities for students to pursue their interests?

_____ Does your school use individual learning plans for academically advanced, gifted students, and/or gifted students with disabilities?

COLLABORATION

_____ Does the collaborative RtI team include educators in gifted education?

_____ Do administrators in your district support the inclusion of gifted or academically advanced students in the RtI model?

_____ Do all teachers receive professional development that includes information about advanced students and evidence-based strategies in gifted education to meet their needs?

Figure 6.1. Assessing your school's RtI model.

OVERALL MODEL: FLEXIBLE PROBLEM-SOLVING APPROACH

RtI models need to be based on high-quality, research-based instruction and interventions. In other words, educators must use methods and materials and make decisions that are guided by research. The curriculum doesn't necessarily have to be commercially prepared as long as it incorporates evidence-based practices such as formative assessment, explicit instruction related to the assessment, appropriate level of challenge, opportunities to respond and practice, and immediate feedback (Crawford & Snider, 2000; Foorman, Francis, & Fletcher, 1998; Fuchs & Fuchs, 1986; National Research Council, 2000). For gifted learners, the curriculum needs to be differentiated, with students learning content that has depth and complexity, accelerating at a pace that matches their knowledge and skills, and using multiple avenues to show mastery (Kaplan, 2005; Rogers, 2002; Tomlinson, 1999, 2005).

Unfortunately, some teachers have experienced the implementation of a rigid "RtI curriculum," one that is scripted and provides for little variation for individual students. Gifted students are sometimes held hostage in a classroom where the results from formative assessments showing their advanced progress are ignored, and they are required to participate in a group lesson because it is part of the standard protocol or the core curriculum.

On the other hand, the implementation of a more flexible approach has the potential of identifying gifted and talented students who need early intervention, particularly those who have disabilities, who are from lower income backgrounds, or who are English language learners. A diagnostic-prescriptive approach can focus on both strengths and weaknesses, whether it is in a standard protocol or problem-solving model (Bellack & Hersen, 1990; Deno & Mirkin, 1977; Morrison & Rizza, 2007; Stanley, 1978). In this approach, a problem-solving team identifies and defines the problem/goal, designs and implements interventions, monitors the results, and continues the intervention until the problem is solved and/or the goal is met. For example, a kindergarten student who is reading at the fourth-grade level is identified by the problem-solving team. The team sets an educational goal of engaging her in reading a variety of non-fiction and novels independently. Her kindergarten classroom teacher implements the goal and monitors her progress. If she is progressing well with the fourth-grade standards, she continues; if she needs more or less acceleration, modifications are made.

In the case of a gifted student with learning disabilities, a multidimensional assessment approach with individualized plans and interdisciplinary consulting teams may be used (Morrison & Rizza, 2007). In this case, the fifth-grade student's strengths in science and weaknesses in writing are identified. The student is provided advanced opportunities for studying science with a group of students with gifts and talents who share common interests. Depending on the extent of the weakness in writing or the severity of the disability, she receives specific instruction to develop her writing skills from her classroom teacher or from the special education teacher.

In summary, to serve gifted students, the overall RtI model needs to be flexible and allow a problem-solving approach that addresses both strengths and weaknesses. This flexibility is particularly important for gifted students who often have asynchronous development (i.e., uneven development in academic, social, physical, and emotional areas) and for those with disabilities who may be overlooked during the assessment process.

MONITORING STUDENT PROGRESS: CONTINUAL ASSESSMENT OF STRENGTHS AND WEAKNESSES

Because it is difficult to know if an intervention is working without assessing its effects, another important component of RtI models is the monitoring of student progress (Bolt, 2005; Johnson & Smith, 2008). For the most part, within most RtI models, monitoring occurs for struggling students but not for advanced students. Three important pieces are needed to make sure that gifted students are included in the monitoring process. First, monitoring needs to focus on both strengths and weaknesses. Is the school looking for students who are above grade level as well as below grade level in specific academic areas? Are advanced learners able to accelerate in a talent area? Are students with learning disabilities who also have gifts and talents identified?

The second piece, which is highly related to the first one, is the use of adequate assessments. Assessments need to have enough ceiling so that gifted students can show what they know as well as what they don't know (Lupkowski-Shoplik & Assouline, 1993; Lupkowski-Shoplik & Swiatek, 1999; Montana Office of Public Instruction, 2009). If a student knows all of the information on a preassessment, then above-grade-level assessments should be used to provide information about what knowledge and skills the student doesn't know. These assessments may include running records, specific academic probes, checklists, work samples, portfolios, achievement tests, student interviews, and curriculum-based measures. For gifted students with disabilities, they may perform above grade level on some assessments and below grade level on others, so results need to be profiled instead of collapsed into a single summary (Brody & Mills, 1997). For example, an achievement test with multiple subtests may show above-grade-level performance in one area (e.g., reading) and below-grade-level performance in another (e.g., math). In this case, the teacher may want to conduct additional probes to identify how advanced the student might be in reading (e.g., using above-grade-level reading materials) or what specific areas of weakness might be evident in the math area (e.g., specific skills at or below grade level).

The final piece relates to the frequency of the assessment. With continual or dynamic assessment, the teacher may find those students who are not only at risk but who are also learning new information quickly (Borland & Wright, 1994; Johnsen, 1997; Kirschenbaum, 1998). These types of data are highly relevant for gifted children from lower income backgrounds or English language learners who may not demonstrate much knowledge initially, but as they acquire the language or have opportunities for learning, their growth rates surpass other children in the classroom and the need for a modified, accelerated curriculum becomes evident.

In summary, the monitoring process needs to focus on both strengths and weaknesses, use assessments that have enough ceiling for gifted students, and be continual or dynamic to identify gifted students who often do not receive gifted programming such as those from lower income backgrounds, English language learners, and those with disabilities.

TIERED LEVELS OF SERVICE: VARIED INTERVENTIONS BASED ON NEEDS NOT LABELS

The primary emphasis within a tiered-level model is based on each student's need rather than his or her label (Cummings, Atkins, Allison, & Cole, 2008; Deno, 1989; Pereles, Omdal, & Baldwin, 2009; Shinn, 1995). In other words, the teacher and the student support team are not trying to place students in particular categories but are implementing a variety of interventions to assist the student in learning new knowledge and skills.

Within each tier of supportive educational interventions, certain school practices need to be in place to ensure that gifted and talented students' needs are met. In the *first tier* where universal screening occurs, above-grade-level knowledge and skills need to be incorporated into the assessments so that gifted students' strengths are evident (Hughes & Rollins, 2009). For students to accelerate as needed, assessments need to be linked to a rigorous curriculum. Flexible, homogeneous grouping is also used as needed for differentiation within the general education classroom (Montana Office of Public Instruction, 2009). If the RtI model doesn't provide for differentiated instruction with aligned above-grade-level assessments, then the school will have difficulty in identifying gifted students who need academic acceleration and more complex content.

Within the *second tier*, varied interventions beyond the general education classroom are needed for the gifted student to succeed (Rollins, Mursky, Shah-Coltrane, & Johnsen, 2009). Gifted students may need to (a) be served with other gifted students at their grade level or at higher grade levels, (b) receive specialized curriculum that has been developed for gifted and academically able students to address their talents, (c) conduct independent studies, (d) be guided by a mentor, and/or (e) participate in out-of-school learning opportunities or competitions with other gifted students. In the case of gifted students with disabilities, they may need to receive interventions from both special and gifted education teachers with specific skill instruction in their areas of weakness and modifications to the specialized curriculum in their areas of strength (Pereles et al., 2009).

Within the *third tier*, more intensive services are needed to support the gifted student such as radical acceleration, dual enrollment in college courses, long-term mentorships, or specialized classrooms or schools (Rollins et al., 2009). Similar to the second tier, a student who is gifted and also has a severe disability may receive concurrent services from special education and gifted education in specialized settings. This level of service may involve more comprehensive assessments for identification purposes. However, the assessments should focus on both strengths and weaknesses to identify student need.

In conclusion, tiers of service need the involvement of general, special, and gifted educators. Each tier requires a variety of differentiated assessments, curricula, and interventions that are matched to each student's strengths and weaknesses.

CURRICULUM AND INSTRUCTIONAL PRACTICES: DIFFERENTIATED AND INDIVIDUALIZED

Differentiation needs to occur at each tier so that curriculum and instructional practices are adapted to student needs. To determine who needs differentiation, the Heartland Education Agency (Schmidt, Moehring, Robinson, & Harken, n.d.) suggested that a teacher ask these questions: What am I teaching? Who knows it? Who can learn it faster? Who needs complexity and abstraction? If a teacher does respond affirmatively to these questions, what does he or she do? What does high-quality, research-based differentiation look like at each tier?

According to Tomlinson (2005), high-quality differentiated curriculum is paced according to each student's rate of learning so that students do not have to wait for others to catch up or engage in tangential, superficial activities or more of the same (Rogers, 2002; Southern & Jones, 1991). Rather, they have opportunities to accelerate into above-grade-level content or delve deeper in areas that interest them. Second, the curriculum is moderately challenging so that with assistance, the student is able to learn new information (National Research Council, 2000; Vygotsky, 1978). Challenge may involve depth and complexity of study; the use of rules, language, and tools of the discipline; a focus on ethical dilemmas and unsolved problems in a field of study; examining individual or disciplinary perspectives about topics and issues; detecting patterns, trends, and big ideas within and across disciplines (Kaplan, 1994, 2005); and developing advanced skills of independent study (Betts, 1985; Johnsen & Johnson, 2007). Finally, differentiated curriculum develops and addresses the students' interests so that they extend their studies in their areas of passion (Bloom, 1985; Csikszentmihalyi, Rathunde, & Whalen, 1993; Renzulli & Reis, 1997). All of these qualities are "rooted in good curriculum and instruction and proceed from there in ways that extends the learner cognitively and affectively" (Tomlinson, 2005, p. 165).

Therefore, at each tier, high-quality, research-based differentiation occurs. The location may vary (e.g., general education classroom, special group, special class, special school); the peer group may vary (e.g., grade level, above grade level, other gifted peers); the degree of differentiation may vary (e.g., radical acceleration, early entry to college, extended studies with professionals in a field); and the uniqueness of the individual student's program may vary (e.g., individualized learning or educational plan). Flexibility is needed within the RtI model so that each student receives the appropriate curriculum and instructional modifications to enhance their growth.

COLLABORATION: A TEAM OF GENERAL, SPECIAL, AND GIFTED EDUCATORS AND OTHER STAKEHOLDERS

Collaborative problem solving across school personnel and with families is key to the inclusion of gifted students within the RtI model (Coleman & Hughes, 2009). Because RtI is interpreted as providing supports for struggling learners only, most often the team includes only general and special educators. The inclusion of educators who have special training in gifted education would be a necessary addition to most schools' RtI models to implement more inclusionary RtI practices.

Within each layer or tier of intervention, members of the team ensure that seamless levels of support exist among and across tiers, making decisions about the most appropriate education for struggling and/or advanced learners (Hoover & Patton, 2008; Rollins et al., 2009). Hoover and Patton (2008) identified five key roles of team members: data-driven decision maker, implementing evidence-based interventions, differentiating instruction, implementing socioemotional and behavioral supports, and collaborating. Table 6.1 shows the knowledge and skills that would be associated with each of these key roles for special, general, and gifted educators (Crone & Horner, 2003; Hoover & Patton, 2005, 2008; Idol, 2002; Kitano, Montgomery, VanTassel-Baska, & Johnsen, 2008; Moran & Malott, 2004; Robinson, Shore, & Enersen, 2007; VanTassel-Baska & Johnsen, 2007; Vaughn & Fuchs, 2003).

If gifted students are included in the RtI process, *all* educators who assume these roles and collaborate with others in a problem-solving team will need professional development in the areas identified in Table 6.1, which include the characteristics of gifted students and the curriculum and instructional strategies that are effective with them.

Effective interventions for gifted students would also require administrators' support of incorporating gifted students within the school's RtI model. The National Association of State Directors of Special Education (Kurns & Tilly, 2008) has developed a blueprint for implementing RtI at the school-building level, which includes ways of building consensus,

TABLE 6.1
KNOWLEDGE AND SKILLS ASSOCIATED
WITH GIFTED, GENERAL, AND
SPECIAL EDUCATOR ROLES

Role	Knowledge and Skills
Data-driven decision maker	• Curriculum-based measurement (above and below grade level) • Ceiling effects • Varied types of assessments • Monitoring strategies • Data analysis (strengths and weaknesses) • Using formative and preassessment information for instructional planning • Eligibility criteria for gifted and special education
Implementing evidence-based interventions	• Knowledge of characteristics of gifted and special education students • Knowledge of core disciplines within and across grade levels • Specialized/alternative curriculum for gifted and special education students • Complex content • Evidence-based instructional strategies • Task analysis and direct instruction • Flexible grouping • Mastery learning • Radical acceleration • Dual enrollment • Independent studies • Out-of-school learning and mentorships • Functional living and transition skills • Impact of culture and language on learning
Differentiating instruction	• Modifications and accommodations • Assistive technologies • Second language acquisition • Higher level thinking and metacognitive models • Acceleration • Challenging curriculum • Advanced skills of independent study • Developing students' interests • Culturally responsive instruction • Study skills and learning strategies • Targeted academic learning time • Scheduling and instructional management strategies

TABLE 6.1, CONTINUED

Implementing socio- emotional and behavioral supports	• Classroom management • Behavior management • Applied behavior analysis • Social skills instruction • Self-management and self-regulation • Impact of culture and language on behavior • Social and emotional development • Development of independence, interdependence, and positive peer relationships • Functional behavior assessment • Positive behavior supports

building infrastructure, and implementing the RtI process. Important elements are communication across all stakeholders, building human and material resources and supports, developing a leadership team, providing professional development, using data to make informed decisions, and monitoring and evaluating the implementation of the process. Throughout this blueprint, gifted and talented students are specifically mentioned,

> Share the message with persons representing many different educational components (e.g., general education; curriculum; administration; Title 1; gifted and talented; English language learners and special education). This will convey the message that RtI is not a special education initiative; it is an ALL education initiative. (Kurns & Tilly, 2008, p. 9)

In conclusion, collaboration involves all educators, including those with specialties in gifted education. Because of the diverse set of knowledge and skills required, professional development is key to the implementation of a successful RtI model. Administrators can assist with its implementation by carefully attending to the school's infrastructure, leadership, and needed human and material resources.

SUMMARY

RtI is a process that has the potential for recognizing and addressing the needs of both special education and gifted students. For gifted students to be included, differentiation needs to occur at all tiers with a flexible problem-solving approach that involves teams of general, special, and gifted educators and other stakeholders. These teams would implement research-based, quality interventions that would be based on an individual student's needs. They would ensure that assessments are differentiated, have sufficient ceiling, and examine each student's strengths and weaknesses. They would collect and analyze data and develop plans so that each student succeeds.

In examining your school's RtI model, the more times you answered "yes" to each of the questions in Figure 6.1, the more likely it is that you may have a model in your school that is inclusionary of gifted and talented students. However, if your model focuses primarily on students with disabilities, you may want to involve stakeholders who might be able to broaden the focus of the services. Use this checklist to begin the conversation.

REFERENCES

Bellack, A. S., & Hersen, M. (1990). *Behavioral consultation in applied settings: An individual guide*. New York, NY: Plenum Press.

Betts, G. (1985). *Autonomous Learner Model for the gifted and talented*. Greeley, CO: ALPS.

Bloom, B. (1985). *Developing talent in young people*. New York, NY: Ballantine.

Bolt, S. E. (2005). Reflections on practice within the Heartland Problem-Solving Model: The perceived value of direct assessment of student needs. *The California School Psychologist, 10,* 65–79.

Borland, J. H., & Wright, L. (1994). Identifying young potentially gifted, economically disadvantaged students. *Gifted Child Quarterly, 38,* 164–171.

Brody, L. E., & Mills, C. J. (1997). Gifted children with learning disabilities: A review of the issues. *Journal of Learning Disabilities, 30,* 282–296.

Coleman, M. R., & Hughes, C. E. (2009). Meeting the needs of gifted students within an RtI framework. *Gifted Child Today, 32*(3), 14–17.

Crawford, D., & Snider, V. E. (2000). Effective mathematics instruction: The importance of curriculum. *Education and Treatment of Children, 23,* 122–142.

Crone, D. A., & Horner, R. H. (2003). *Building positive behavior support systems in schools: Functional behavior assessment*. New York, NY: Guilford.

Csikszentmihalyi, M., Rathunde, K., & Whalen, S. (1993). *Talented teenagers: The roots of success and failure*. New York, NY: Cambridge University Press.

Cummings, K. D., Atkins, T., Allison, R., & Cole, C. (2008). Investigating the new role of special educators. *Teaching Exceptional Children, 40*(4), 24–31.

Deno, S. L. (1989). Curriculum-based measurement and special education services: A fundamental and direct relationship. In M. R. Shinn (Ed.), *Curriculum-based measurement: Assessing special children* (pp. 1–17). New York, NY: Guilford.

Deno, S. L., & Mirkin, P. K. (1977). *Data-based program modification: A manual*. Reston, VA: Council for Exceptional Children.

Foorman, B. R., Francis, D. J., & Fletcher, J. M. (1998). The role of instruction in learning to read: Preventing reading failure in at-risk children. *Journal of Educational Psychology, 90*, 37–55.

Fuchs, L. S., & Fuchs, D. (1986). Effects of systematic formative evaluation: A meta-analysis. *Exceptional Children, 53*, 199–208.

Hoover, J. J., & Patton, J. R. (2005). *Curriculum adaptations for students with learning and behavior problems: Differentiating instruction to meet diverse needs* (3rd. ed.). Austin, TX: Pro-Ed.

Hoover, J. J., & Patton, J. R. (2008). The role of special educators in a multitiered instructional system. *Intervention in School and Clinic, 43*, 195–202.

Hughes, C. E., & Rollins, K. (2009). RtI for nurturing giftedness: Implications for the RtI school-based team. *Gifted Child Today, 32*(3), 31–39.

Idol, L. (2002). *Creating collaborative and inclusive schools*. Austin, TX: Pro-Ed.

Johnsen, S. K. (1997). Assessment beyond definitions. *Peabody Journal of Education, 72*, 137–153.

Johnsen, S. K., & Johnson, K. (2007). *Independent study program* (2nd ed.). Waco, TX: Prufrock Press.

Johnson, E. S., & Smith, L. (2008). Implementation of Response to Intervention at middle school: Challenges and potential benefits. *Exceptional Children, 39*, 46–52.

Kaplan, S. (1994). *Differentiating core curriculum and instruction to provide advanced learning opportunities*. Sacramento, CA: California Association for the Gifted.

Kaplan, S. K. (2005). Layering differentiated curriculum for the gifted and talented. In F. A. Karnes & S. M. Bean (Eds.), *Methods and materials for teaching the gifted* (2nd ed., pp. 107–132). Waco, TX: Prufrock Press.

Kirschenbaum, R. (1998). Dynamic assessment and its use with underserved gifted and talented populations. *Gifted Child Quarterly, 42*, 140–147.

Kitano, M., Montgomery, D., VanTassel-Baska, J., & Johnsen, S. (2008).

Using the national gifted education standards for PreK–12 professional development. Thousand Oaks, CA: Corwin Press.

Kurns, S., & Tilly, W. D. (2008). *Response to Intervention blueprints: School building level edition.* Alexandria, VA: National Association of State Directors of Special Education.

Lupkowski-Shoplik, A., & Assouline, S. G. (1993). Identifying mathematically talented elementary students: Using the lower level of the SSAT. *Gifted Child Quarterly, 37,* 118–123.

Lupkowski-Shoplik, A., & Swiatek, M. A. (1999). Elementary student talent searches: Establishing appropriate guidelines for qualifying test scores. *Gifted Child Quarterly, 43,* 265–272.

Montana Office of Public Instruction. (2009). *Response to Intervention and gifted and talented education.* Helena, MT: Author. Retrieved from opi.mt.gov/Resources/RTI/Index.html

Moran, D. J., & Malott, R. W. (2004). *Evidence-based educational methods.* Boston, MA: Elsevier Academic Press.

Morrison, W. F., & Rizza, M. G. (2007).Creating a toolkit for identifying twice-exceptional students. *Journal for the Education of the Gifted, 31,* 57–76.

National Research Council. (2000). *How people learn: Brain, mind, experience, and school.* Washington, DC: National Academy Press.

Pereles, D. A., Omdal, S., & Baldwin, L. (2009). Response to Intervention and twice-exceptional learners: A promising fit. *Gifted Child Today, 32*(3), 40–51.

Renzulli, J., & Reis, S. (1997). *The Schoolwide Enrichment Model: A comprehensive plan for educational excellence* (2nd ed.). Mansfield Center, CT: Creative Learning Press.

Robinson, A., Shore, B. M., & Enersen, D. L. (2007). *Best practices in gifted education: An evidence-based guide.* Waco, TX: Prufrock Press.

Rogers, K. B. (2002). *Re-forming gifted education: How parents and teachers can match the program to the child.* Scottsdale, AZ: Great Potential Press.

Rollins, K., Mursky, C. V., Shah-Coltrane, S., & Johnsen, S. K. (2009). RtI models for gifted children. *Gifted Child Today, 32*(3), 20–30.

Schmidt, M., Moehring, L., Robinson, W., & Harken, S. (n.d.).

Instructional decision making: Session 4: Advanced proficiency. Johnston, IA: Heartland Area Education Agency 11.

Shinn, M. R. (1995). Best practices in curriculum-based measurement and its use in a problem-solving model. In A. Thomas & J. Grimes (Eds.), *Best practices in school psychology III* (pp. 547–567). Silver Spring, MD: National Association of School Psychologists.

Southern, W. T., & Jones, E. (Eds.). (1991). *Academic acceleration of gifted children.* New York, NY: Teachers College Press.

Stanley, J. C. (1978). SMPY's DT/PI mentor model: Diagnostic testing followed by prescriptive instruction. *Intellectually Talented Youth Bulletin, 4*(10), 7–8.

Tomlinson, C. A. (1999). *The differentiated classroom: Responding to the needs of all learners.* Alexandria, VA: Association for Supervision and Curriculum Development.

Tomlinson, C. A. (2005). Quality curriculum and instruction for highly able students. *Theory Into Practice, 44,* 160–166.

VanTassel-Baska, J., & Johnsen, S. K. (2007). Teacher education standards for the field of gifted education: A vision of coherence for personnel preparation in the 21st century. *Gifted Child Quarterly, 51,* 182–205.

Vaughn, S., & Fuchs, L. S. (2003). Redefining learning disabilities as inadequate response to instruction: The promise and potential problems. *Learning Disabilities Research & Practice, 18,* 137–146.

Vygotsky, L. (1978). *Mind in society.* Cambridge, MA: Harvard University Press.

CHAPTER 7

Challenges for Including Gifted Education Within an RtI Model

Claire E. Hughes, Karen Rollins,
Susan K. Johnsen, Daphne Pereles,
Stuart Omdal, Lois Baldwin, Elissa F. Brown,
Sherry H. Abernethy, and Mary Ruth Coleman

In the Summer 2009 special issue of *Gifted Child Today* and in preparation for this book, contributing authors were asked to think about the challenges faced if gifted education moves toward an RtI approach. These shared challenges can be used as discussion points for planning and reflection.

CHALLENGES FOR RTI

In reviewing the challenges, we categorized them under three headings: RtI as Systemic Change, Implementing RtI in Schools and

Classrooms, and Specific Implementation Issues for Twice-Exceptional Students.

RTI AS SYSTEMIC CHANGE

Response to Intervention has many positive features that will help students not only succeed, but when paired with a strand that incorporates gifted education, could even help students reach their potential. However, RtI will not be successful unless it is viewed as a systemic process that involves systemic change. For change to occur at the classroom level, it must also involve administrative support at the school and district levels. If implementation is not done systemically, RtI will meet with limited success.

Program intent and philosophy. Employing RtI as a framework for gifted programming requires that programming be inclusive rather than exclusive because of the emphasis on universal screening and proactively responding to students' needs based on formative and curriculum-based assessment. Many gifted programs and state policies still operate with an "exclusivity" model wherein only students whose aptitude or achievement scores fall within a range above the mean can receive services. Using an RtI model to design policy would challenge assumptions around narrow definitions and identification processes for determining who is gifted and would include the nurturing of potential as part of the services. A challenge for gifted education teachers and administrators is adjusting to a major change in the identification process. For decades the first step in the gifted education process was identifying who was and was not "gifted." The label became the key to services and programming. When students display the characteristics and/or behaviors associated with giftedness and the school system is poised to respond to those documented academic needs for enrichment and/or acceleration, the need for the gifted label is no longer the gatekeeper to services and programming associated with gifted and talented education.

Budget and resource implications. If gifted education employs an RtI approach, there are budget implications for teacher preparation, curriculum and assessment materials, program implementation, and program evaluation. Given current budgetary constraints for gifted funding in federal and state budgets, allocating money for gifted education remains a challenge. New and collaborative approaches to funding will have to be developed to ensure resources for nurturing, recognizing, and responding to the strengths of all children. Collaborative approaches might include resources from (a) Title I enrichment funds, (b) technology funds for distance learning, (c) media center funds for challenging learning materials, (d) curriculum funds for rigorous high-end classes, and (e) special education or 504 funds for twice-exceptional learners. Just as greater collaboration is needed for service delivery, greater collaboration is also needed to pool resources and reduce the fragmentation of supports.

Leadership. When establishing RtI on a campus, all personnel and all departments must work together in a cohesive fashion in order for the process to work. Most importantly, administration must provide good leadership in order to encourage and foster change. This leadership must come from not only district administrators such as superintendents, curriculum specialists, and special program directors, but also from principals, vice principals, and campus leaders. RtI is a complex system that requires vision, strong leadership, and collaboration. Granted, all personnel must do their part in establishing the system and working with students, but it is the job of administrators to facilitate the change and problem solve for the campus every step of the way.

Professional development. Staff will need training on differentiated instruction and enrichment strategies to enhance instruction for students identified as gifted. Teachers will need an understanding of how to expand curriculum to challenge these identified learners. Additionally, school leaders must have training and commitment to the approach as a way to scaffold learning for all learners. RtI training and long-term follow up will also be an essential component of expanding the capacity to support the change.

IMPLEMENTING RTI IN SCHOOLS AND CLASSROOMS

Educators who implement RtI in schools and in classrooms face special challenges that relate to differentiating Tier 1, collaborating with other professionals and parents, identifying research-based practices in gifted education, developing decision points for more intensive services, and finding or developing appropriate assessment tools and strategies.

Implementing differentiated strategies within Tier 1. For RtI to be responsive to gifted and talented students, differentiation needs to occur at the Tier 1 level in all core subject areas. In this way, students who have strengths in one subject area and who exhibit a disability in another may receive appropriate interventions. In the case of gifted students, these interventions might include adding depth and complexity to the content, faster pacing, independent study, choices among assignments, above-grade-level activities, curriculum compacting, tiered assignments, and so on. It is not easy for teachers to provide for a wide range of differences in the classroom. Teachers need to have flexibility in their curriculum and in the activities that they use in the classroom. A standard curriculum will not address each student's strengths and weaknesses. Therefore, teachers need to have access to a variety of curricular materials so that they can intervene with individual students.

Collaboration. Administrators, special education teachers, gifted education teachers, and other support personnel need to assist the general education teacher in implementing varied interventions and in reviewing the assessment information to determine their effectiveness. Moreover, this support needs to be ongoing and help the teacher learn how to manage a wide range of differences in the classroom. Management techniques might include the use of flexible grouping, a variety of activities, student record keeping, learning stations, flexible pacing and scheduling, and independent studies. With curricular and instructional support, there is a greater likelihood that appropriate support can occur at the Tier 1 level and all students will receive instruction that adapts to their abilities and disabilities.

Research-based instructional practices. In both RtI approaches for special education students (i.e., standard protocol and problem solving), there is an emphasis on research-based practices so that students who need more intensive services or services beyond the general education classroom actually need them—and not because they received inadequate instruction. Just as in special education, gifted education needs to clearly identify practices that have evidence to support their use. In gifted education, several books have been written regarding best practices (Callahan & Plucker, 2008; Robinson, Shore, & Enersen, 2007). These books address a variety of areas that include topics such as flexible grouping, compacting the curriculum, higher level thinking, and instructional strategies within specific curriculum domains. The Council for Exceptional Children (2008) has also initiated a project for analyzing and determining which evidence should be used to support a particular practice. They have developed criteria for reviewing articles that use specific research designs. As practices are validated, they plan to disseminate these to schools and teachers. Teachers may also choose to take an active role in developing an evidence base by using action research in their classroom. Action research involves problem solving similar to the RtI approach. Baseline information is collected on a student's academic or behavioral progress, an intervention is applied, more data are collected, and decisions are made about the effectiveness of the intervention. If the intervention is working, it is continued; if not, another intervention is implemented. Action research has the potential to generate new effective interventions for all students.

Research support enables the teacher to select the most effective programs, materials, and instructional strategies for gifted students. The challenge for those involved in research is getting these best practices into the hands of teachers who provide direct services to students. Too frequently, curriculum and instructional strategies are based upon opinion, habit, or tradition. To encourage more data-based decision making when interventions are selected, researchers need to make their results more accessible to practitioners. Similarly, practitioners need to ask the question: Is there any research evidence to support this practice?

Developing decision points for more intensive services. Among educators, a major issue is determining the point when students need more intensive services. When does the teacher refer a child for special education or for gifted education? What constitutes inadequate progress or progress that requires more than what the general education classroom can provide? What assessments should be used in this more comprehensive level of evaluation? Highly gifted students may need radical acceleration (e.g., even though they are elementary students, they are ready to learn calculus), intensive counseling (e.g., they are very different in terms of their interests and maturity from their same-age peers), or other out-of-school activities (e.g., mentoring, competitions, dual-enrollment options). Decision-making guidelines must be created that include these kinds of high-end options.

Changes in assessment. Progress monitoring to determine needs in intensity of instruction and strategies will be required when implementing an RtI model. Appropriate assessment tools and strategies will need to be identified to determine accelerated knowledge and potential growth of gifted students. This will require the general education teacher to use assessments that are above grade level. Such assessments are not commonly used because state-mandated tests are tightly aligned to grade-level expectations. The inclusion of above-grade-level assessments or those that assess what gifted students know is a challenge within the RtI model. To be truly useful, teachers will need assessment data documenting when a child has progressed well beyond the expected classroom curriculum. In addition, assessments should help formally identified students so that resources can be provided for more intensive services.

SPECIFIC IMPLEMENTATION ISSUES FOR TWICE-EXCEPTIONAL STUDENTS

Concurrently with modifications that address their individual strengths and interests, gifted students with disabilities should also be receiving interventions that directly impact the area in which they are experiencing difficulty. This dual set of needs complicates identification and service delivery; therefore, the following specific concerns are noted for RtI with twice-exceptional learners:

- If the school system is not utilizing RtI as a comprehensive system for all students, then academic acceleration would not be part of the potential options in the screening/intervention process. This can be a problem, not only for gifted students but especially for twice-exceptional students.
- If the system is only focused on "struggling learners," then there will be a tendency to focus on the remedial needs of twice-exceptional students rather than putting a critical emphasis on their abilities.

- Lack of awareness of the characteristics of twice-exceptional students can greatly impact whether the academic, social, and emotional needs of these students are addressed.
- Because their gifts and higher level thinking often masks their disability, twice-exceptional students may appear to be very average in the classroom setting. The expectation is that schoolwide screening for strengths and interests as well as academic challenges would identify possible concerns. If the classroom teacher does not observe any perceived problems, as in the potential for much higher achievement, or below-grade-level expectations in an academic subject, the student may never be referred to the problem-solving team.
- Many twice-exceptional students get noticed because of their negative behaviors. This can cause a focus on the behavior rather than the underlying academic problem that may be contributing to the negative behavior. It can also interfere with any recognition of students' abilities or gifts.
- If the process is done with fidelity and includes a strength-based approach, these issues should not be a concern. But, the fidelity of implementation is inconsistent at best.

CONCLUDING THOUGHTS ON CHALLENGES FOR RTI WITH GIFTED EDUCATION

Change is a difficult process, and systemic change is even more difficult. Roles and responsibilities will change. Questions without answers will be asked. Parents and students will need to be informed. An administrator who can listen, empathize, and foster energy will go far with the implementation of RtI. As long as there is positive energy and successful leadership in place, the systemic change can at least be less painful, and the rewards reaped—such as happier, successful students—will be worth the effort.

Questions that may need to be explored to facilitate the systemic change of RtI include these:

- What RtI framework will provide the blueprint of change?
- How will the current services for gifted learners fit with this framework?
- How will roles and responsibilities change?
- How can anxieties about the systemic change be eased?
- What levels of collaboration need to be established?
- How will the needs of high-potential children from culturally and linguistically diverse and economically disadvantaged families be addressed?
- How will long-term follow up for students be provided and by whom?
- How will parents be informed of changes?
- Who will be the "go to" person when questions arise?

In spite of the remaining challenges, the authors conclude that RtI is certainly changing the face of education and that gifted education must examine its fit with these changes.

REFERENCES

Callahan, C. M., & Plucker, J. (2008). *Critical issues and practices in gifted education*. Waco, TX: Prufrock Press.

Council for Exceptional Children. (2008). *Classifying the state of evidence for special education professional practices: CEC practice study manual*. Washington, DC: Author.

Robinson, A., Shore, B. M., & Enersen, D. L. (2007). *Best practices in gifted education: An evidence-based guide*. Waco, TX: Prufrock Press.

CHAPTER 8

RtI Online Resources

The following is a list of websites that have resources for implementing Response to Intervention.

Intervention Central (http://www.interventioncentral.org)

This site provides links to products, academic and behavioral resources, curriculum-based measurements (CBMs), and workshops for RtI. Some of the most popular CBMs include math worksheets, behavior report cards, CBM reading fluency, early math fluency, CBM wordlist fluency, and classroom intervention generators.

The National Center on Response to Intervention (http://rti4success. org)

This center's mission is to provide technical assistance and dissemination about proven and promising models for RtI and Early Intervening Services (EIS) to state and local educators, families, and other stakeholders. The center provides service in four areas: (a) knowledge production, which involves a Technical Review Committee of experts who will independently evaluate the scientific rigor, conditions for successful implementation, and the cultural and linguistic competence of all identified models (and components); (b) implementation supports, which involve training and follow-up activities to scale-up RTI and EIS on a broad scale; (c) information dissemination, which involves forming communities of practice to improve the likelihood that consumers will adopt RtI models; and (d) formative evaluation, which involves an assessment of the quality, implementation, impact, and cost effectiveness of the services offered.

The Iris Center (http://iris.peabody.vanderbilt.edu)

This center is funded by the U.S. Department of Education's Office of Special Education Programs (OSEP) and develops training enhancement materials for faculty and professional development materials. The center works with experts to create challenge-based interactive modules, case study units, and a variety of activities that provide research-validated information about working with students with disabilities in inclusive settings. Fuchs and Fuchs are professors at Vanderbilt University and are two of the most prolific and influential people in RtI today.

Institute of Education Sciences What Works Clearinghouse (http://www.whatworks.ed.gov)

This website reviews research on programs to examine their effects on students. For example, a recent guide on *Using Student Achievement Data to Support Instructional Decision Making* offers five recommendations to help educators effectively use data to monitor students' academic progress and evaluate instructional practices.

National Center on Student Progress Monitoring (http://www.studentprogress.org)

This site contains charts, graphs, and probes for progress monitoring and has downloadable articles, PowerPoint presentations, frequently asked questions documents, screening resources, and information on curriculum-based measurement, applying decision making to IEPs, and other researched-based topics. All publications are designed to inform and assist educators in implementing student progress monitoring at the classroom, building, local, or state level. In addition, the center has established a standard process to evaluate the scientific rigor of commercially available tools to monitor students' progress.

PALS: Phonological Awareness Literacy Screening
(http://pals.virginia.edu)

The Curry School at the University of Virginia provides links to tools, resources, research and development, RtI quick checks, and information for parents at this website. The site also provides information about a screening, diagnostic, and progress monitoring tool for measuring the fundamental components of literacy, which can be purchased.

IDEA Partnership (http://ideapartnership.org)

The IDEA Partnership is funded through the Research to Practice Division of the federal Office of Special Education Programs (OSEP) and is part of OSEP's National Technical Assistance and Dissemination Network. Resources related to RtI include essential elements, assumptions, and guiding principles; a glossary; needs of the field; and PowerPoint presentations and presenters' dialogue guides for sharing information about RtI.

Reading Rockets (http://www.readingrockets.org)

The Reading Rockets project, which is funded by the Office of Special Education of the U.S. Department of Education, is comprised of PBS television programs, online services, and professional development opportunities. The website provides resources about how to teach reading to struggling readers, reading guides, research reports, reading probes, readability formulas, book suggestions, and much more.

RTI Action Network (http://rtinetwork.org)

RTI Action Network is a program of the National Center for Learning Disabilities and is funded by the Cisco Foundation. The site provides descriptions about RtI, how to develop and implement an RtI plan in a school district, professional development activities, video examples from school districts, and many opportunities to connect with others through discussion boards, blogs, newsletters, and conversations with experts.

National Research Center on Learning Disabilities Resource Kit (http://www.nrcld.org/resource_kit)

The National Research Center on Learning Disabilities (NRCLD) has developed a kit to help you navigate changes related to SLD determination and RtI. All materials in this kit are in the public domain, so authorization to reproduce it in whole or in part is granted. The sections of the kit include general information, tools for change, a getting started manual, an RtI manual, PowerPoint presentations, and parent pages.

National Association of School Psychologists Resources (http://www.nasponline.org/resources/rti/index.aspx)

National Association of School Psychologists (NASP), one of the early adopter groups of RtI, examines assessment issues and provides an excellent source of research and implications for school psychologists. Some of the topics include behavior support, CBM data and decision making, cooperative RtI models, and new roles in RtI.

OSEP Technical Assistance Center on Positive Behavioral Interventions and Supports (http://www.pbis.org)

The center has been established to give schools capacity-building information and technical assistance for identifying, adapting, and sustaining effective schoolwide disciplinary practices. The overall goals of the center are to: (a) identify and enhance knowledge about, and practical demonstration of, schoolwide PBS practices, systems, and outcomes along the three-tiered continuum (primary, secondary, tertiary); and (b) develop, conduct, and evaluate technical assistance and dissemination efforts that allow evidence-based practices to be implemented on a large scale with high durability and effectiveness.

Center for Early Literacy Learning (http://www.earlyliteracylearning. org)

This Center for Early Literacy Learning (CELL) is using a tiered model of intervention approach as part of its conceptual framework in identifying evidence-based practices that promote literacy and language development in young children (ages 0–5). Tier 1 includes literacy-rich learning opportunities that are the contexts for skill acquisition for all young children; Tier 2 includes specific instructional practices that promote literacy learning for all young children; and Tier 3 includes specialized practices for supporting the literacy learning of young children with disabilities or learning difficulties that need more specialized interventions. CELL is currently conducting research syntheses on various practices that promote language and literacy, and will ultimately be developing six practice guide toolkits for practitioners and families that address various age levels (infant, toddler, preschooler), formal and informal practices, different literacy-related competencies (print-related and linguistic processing), and the three tiers of intervention. CELL provides general technical assistance to a wide audience and works intensively with a small number of states.

Council for Exceptional Children (http://www.cec.sped.org)

The Council for Exceptional Children (CEC) is an international professional organization that is dedicated to improving the educational success of individuals with disabilities and/or gifts and talents. It provides webinars and other information related to RtI and other special education topics.

Scientifically Based Research (http://www.gosbr.net)

This site is devoted to sharing proven practices in interventions for reading, math, writing, assessment and screening, and other areas.

Dr. Mac's Behavior Management Site (http://www.behavioradvisor. com)

This site contains lesson plans for teaching behavior management to students, the basics of behavior management, tips for becoming an effective manager, strategies for addressing common behaviors and conditions, ways of assessing and measuring behavior, the applied behavior analysis model and interventions, cognitive behavioral models and interventions, and how to implement a schoolwide behavior management system.

AIMSWeb (http://www.aimsweb.com)

This website provides a benchmark and progress monitoring system that includes benchmarks, monthly monitoring, and individualized progress monitoring. Purchasing information is available at the website.

Joe Witt (http://www.joewitt.org)

Joe Witt, a leading researcher and author on RtI, has established a site that provides resources and information related to instruction and progress monitoring. He includes two papers that review the research on RtI, information about consulting projects, and STEEP, a system to enhance educational performance.

About the Editors

Mary Ruth Coleman, Ph.D., is a senior scientist at the Frank Porter Graham Child Development Institute and Research Associate Professor in the School of Education at the University of North Carolina at Chapel Hill. She directed Project U-STARS~PLUS (Using Science, Talents and Abilities to Recognize Students), a Javits Gifted and Talented Student Education Program and project.

Susan K. Johnsen, Ph.D., is professor in the Department of Educational Psychology at Baylor University. She directs the Ph.D. program and programs related to gifted and talented education. She has written more than 150 articles, monographs, technical reports, and books related to gifted education. She is a frequent presenter at international, national, and state conferences. She is editor of *Gifted Child Today* and editor of *Identifying Gifted Students: A Practical Guide*, coauthor of the *Independent Study Program*, and coauthor of three tests used in identifying gifted students: Test of Mathematical Abilities for Gifted Students (TOMAGS), Test of Nonverbal Intelligence (TONI-4), and Screening Assessment for Gifted Elementary and Middle School Students (SAGES-2). She is president of The Association for the Gifted, Council for Exceptional Children and past-president of the Texas Association for Gifted and Talented.

About the Authors

Sherry H. Abernethy, M.Ed., is the State Consultant for Learning Disabilities and RtI with the North Carolina Department of Public Instruction, Exceptional Children Division. Previously, she worked as an instructional specialist and teacher for students with disabilities.

Lois Baldwin, Ed.D., was the teacher and administrator for the Southern Westchester Board of Cooperative Educational Services in White Plains, NY, the first program for twice-exceptional students in the country. As a national consultant for twice-exceptional learners, Lois has worked with the Colorado Department of Education over the last 3 years to help develop a Level Two twice-exceptional training that is aligned with the state's RtI initiative. She is the cofounder and current president of the national advocacy organization, Association for the Education for Gifted Underachieving Students (AEGUS).

Elissa F. Brown, Ph.D., is the Director for Secondary Projects and recently served as State Consultant for Academically/Intellectually Gifted with the North Carolina Department of Public Instruction. Prior to her recent appointment in North Carolina, she was the director of the Center for Gifted Education at The College of William and Mary.

Claire E. Hughes, Ph.D., is an associate professor of teacher education at the College of Coastal Georgia. She has worked in gifted and special education in grades K–12, taught both undergraduate and graduate programs, and has a particular interest in twice-exceptional children and service implications.

Chrystyna V. Mursky, Ph.D., is State Director for Gifted and Talented Education and Advanced Placement at the Wisconsin Department of Public Instruction. As a member of the agency-wide Response to Intervention leadership team, she is coordinating a collaborative multimedia project on RtI. She has served as a K–12 gifted and talented coordinator and resource teacher and has taught math and science.

Stuart Omdal, Ph.D., is a professor of gifted education in the School of Special Education at the University of Northern Colorado. He is the assistant director of the Center for the Education and Study of Gifted, Talented, Creative Learners and the education director for the Summer Enrichment Program. Interests include the underachievement of high-ability students, the development of appropriate curriculum for high-ability students and the role of creativity in gifted and talented education.

Daphne Pereles, M.S., is the Director for School Improvement & Turnaround, and RtI/PBIS for the Colorado Department of Education. She directs state efforts to assist districts and schools to create educational systems that support increased student achievement for all. The Response to Intervention and Positive Behavior Interventions and Supports initiatives are an integral part of this work. She has been a teacher in general, special, and gifted education as well as a special education coordinator and twice-exceptional specialist for a large suburban district. Daphne has been a board member for the Association for the Education of Gifted Underachieving Students (AEGUS) for the past 10 years.

Karen Rollins, M.S., LPC, is a Licensed Professional Counselor in private practice, specializing in children with disabilities. She is a presenter for the Center for Learning and Development, which focuses on children with learning difficulties and ADHD.

Sneha Shah-Coltrane, M.A., is the State Consultant for Academically/ Intellectually Gifted at the North Carolina Department of Public Instruction. She was formerly the Co-Director of U-STARS~PLUS at the Frank Porter Graham Child Development Institute at UNC-Chapel Hill and has worked with K–5 gifted learners, teachers of the gifted and organizations focused on gifted issues, both locally and nationally.

The Association
for the Gifted

For more than 50 years, The Association for the Gifted (TAG), as a Division of the Council for Exceptional Children (CEC), has been the leading voice for special and gifted education and is devoted to twice-exceptional children, educational excellence, and diversity. CEC-TAG establishes professional standards for teacher preparation for the field, develops initiatives to improve gifted education practice, and ensures that the needs of children and youth with exceptionalities are met in educational legislation. To learn more about TAG and to become an active member, visit http://www.cectag.org.